MARY CLARE CLARK

STORY QUILTS

AND HOW TO MAKE THEM

MARY CLARE CLARK

STORY QUILTS

AND HOW TO MAKE THEM

Introduction by Shelly Zegart
Illustrations by Penny Brown

Sterling Publishing Co., Inc. New York
A Sterling/Museum Quilts Book

Editors: Ljiljana Baird and Annlee Landman
Designer: Bet Ayer and Sonia Alexis

Library of Congress Cataloging-in-Publication Data

Clark, Mary Clare.
　　Story quilts : how to make them / by Mary Clare Clark ;
introduction by Shelly Zegart.
　　　　P.　　cm
　　"A Sterling / Museum Quilts book."
　　Includes index.
　　ISBN 0-8069-1316-9
　　1. Patchwork.　2. Appliqué.　3. Quilts—Themes, motives.
I. Title.
TT835.C567　1995
746.46—dc20　　　　　　　　　　　　　　　　　　　　　　　95-34185
　　　　　　　　　　　　　　　　　　　　　　　　　　　　　　　　　CIP

2 4 6 8 10 9 7 5 3 1

A STERLING/MUSEUM QUILTS BOOK

Published by Sterling Publishing Company, Inc.,
387 Park Avenue South, New York, NY 10016
and by Museum Quilts Publications Inc.
Published in the UK by Museum Quilts (UK) Inc.,
254-258 Goswell Road, London EC1V 7EB
Distributed in Canada by Sterling Publishing
c/o Canadian Manda Group, One Atlantic Avenue, Suite 105
Toronto, Ontario, Canada M6K 3E7
Distributed in Australia by Capricorn Link (Australia) Pty Ltd.,
P.O. Box 6651, Baulkham Hills Business Centre
NSW 2153, Australia

The author has endeavored to ensure that all project instructions are accurate. However, due to variations in readers' individual skill and materials available, neither the author nor the publishers can accept responsibility for damages or losses resulting from the instructions herein. All instructions should be studied and clearly understood before beginning any project.

Printed and bound by ORIENTAL PRESS, DUBAI.

ISBN: 0-8069-1316-9

FRONTISPIECE
(left to right)

1st Row: Pretty Polly; Farmyard; They Came Two by Two
2nd Row: Out Walking; Adam and Eve in the Garden; Along the Garden Path
3rd Row: By the Boating Lake; Floral Fireworks; Gathering in the Grapes
4th Row: Vase Bouquet; Wagon Train; Two Ladies and the Giant Urn

CONTENTS

INTRODUCTION

The quilt, that most anonymous of women's arts, rarely dated or signed, summarizes more than any other form the major themes in a woman's life – its beginnings, endings, and celebrations retold in bits of colored cloth. In bridal quilts, patchwork coverlets for daily use, parlor quilts, "album" quilts (made collectively to honor relatives, friends or local notables) — even in widow's quilts — a woman said everything she knew about art and life.

Mirra Bank, Anonymous Was a Woman, *1979*

Quilts over the centuries have both warmed our bodies and conveyed in every stitch our human experience. Because women are caretakers of family memories, pictorial quilts record and celebrate important relationships and events more than any other type of quilt. They remind us of the care and concern we have for one another. They are windows for us to look back through into another time. Pictorial quilts have, in effect, become textile time capsules. They record both the grand events and the common occurrences of the periods and places in which the makers lived.

For centuries quilting had been mainly a means of holding layers of cloth and batting together to create clothing and bedcovers of exceptional warmth. In the more elaborate works – bodices and petticoats, for example – the stitching was used not only to hold together the layers but to create attractive designs, usually geometric and floral. Such quilted clothing and some bedcovers for the wealthy became more and more elaborate as finer cotton fabrics became available in the late seventeenth and early eighteenth centuries. Some dyed and painted cottons appeared and whetted the appetites for more colorful and complicated designs. The elaborate Indian palampores, or bedspreads, usually depicting the "Tree of Life," were designed to please the taste of the English and French upper classes. Europeans imposed their own ideas on the eastern designers so that the flora and fauna of the western world appeared in the art work of the Near East. It then remained for the needlewomen of Europe to cut out, rearrange, and appliqué these designs on solid cotton backgrounds and then to layer and quilt them into the pieces that can still be seen in museums today.

By the beginning of the nineteenth century other designs and types of quilts appeared in both America and England. One often seen in America at the time was the enormous center design Star of Bethlehem with appliqué designs of the earlier chintz cut-out type filling the corners between the star points. These and other center-medallion quilts were popular through the first thirty or forty years of that century. Sometime after 1840, album quilts with a variety of blocks and designs swept the country from Baltimore to the southern, northern, and western states of America.

The sophisticated Baltimore album quilts have been the subject of much research and endless discussion. Certain names like Mary Evans have been mentioned as the designer-makers of them but recent research has led to more plausible theories. Though the designs for the elaborate baskets of flowers and other themes repeated

Photo: Courtesy of Shelly Zegart

Baltimore Album Quilt, c. 1854, Maryland. Made by Susie Gorrel Harvey and her sister. Private collection

throughout a period of about ten years and dozens of quilts may have been created by one person or one "studio," there are many individual touches in a variety of block designs. Political, religious, and Masonic symbols were popular as well as lighthouses, ships, houses, and personalized items of daily life. This type of quilt design spread throughout the country and appeared in elegant variations in the port cities of Ohio and upstate New York where fine fabrics were available. Even country women created album quilts of more common fabrics using everyday themes of farms, animals, and the silhouettes of children's hands. Spiritual themes and religious symbols often appear, making it possible to detect considerable information about the background of the maker.

Americans were justly proud of their first hundred years as a free country and celebrated their Centennial with the appropriate amount of gusto and patriotism. Yards of fabric were printed with the dates 1776-1876 repeated along with other national symbols and even portraits of presidents and great panels of the Centennial Fairgrounds in Philadelphia. Interestingly, it was the Bicentennial in 1976 that inspired one of the largest quilting revivals that America has ever known after a period of thirty to forty years when the art of quilting had nearly died.

An almost wholly new type of quilt appeared at about the time of

Photo: Courtesy of Shelly Zegart

Centennial Bandanna Quilt, c. 1876, Louisville, Kentucky. Private collection

the Centennial – what we have come to know as the Victorian crazy quilt. There had been some very fine pieced silk quilts earlier in the century, usually in simple geometric patterns, but the silk and velvet crazy quilts, overlaid with embroidery, commemorative ribbons, metallic braid, and lace, were born of the comparatively affluent time of territorial expansion in both America and England. With the growth of the rail system and the coming of luxury ocean travel it was possible to move around between cities and even between countries, go to fairs and other events, and bring back souvenirs and new ideas. Mail order made it possible to acquire fine silks and velvets even in small towns where nothing finer than muslin or calico was sold at the dry-goods store.

The women who made crazy quilts were more often interested in embroidery than in quilting. They loved the elegance of fine fabric and silk embroidery thread and the challenge of inventing more and more complex stitches to embellish the odd-shaped pieces of silk and velvet. There were commercial embroidery motifs of charming little children, bluebirds, and spiders in their webs which appear painstakingly worked throughout many Victorian quilts.

Some of these quilts are elaborately bordered, some trimmed in heavy lace, and some with thick silk cord around the edge. Many were never finished, leading to the reinforcement of the feeling that it was the color, design, and embellishment that fascinated the makers, and there was very little interest in the completion of such basically frivolous items. At best they could be spread across the back of a sofa and admired by guests – certainly not used as a cover at nap time! For today's quilt historian they contain many interesting designs and a number of clues to the politics and travel interests of the makers and their families. As in the case of the album quilts, the influence of the silk and velvet quilts was felt throughout the country and the crazy-quilt idea was translated into wools and even cottons as time went on.

In the early years of the twentieth century factory-made bedcovers and the growing distribution of them through mail-order catalogs threatened to decrease the popularity or at least the necessity of quilt making. However, it did not take long for companies such as *Ladies Art* to counteract this trend with tempting patterns at a very small price.

Soon mail-order companies were selling bundles of print fabric scraps and the magazines such as *Ladies' Home Journal* were publishing quilt patterns by well-known artists of the time. The center medallion appliqué floral designs of artist Rose Kretsinger became very popular and widely imitated. In 1915 Marie Webster wrote a book about quilts and their history (recently published in an enlarged and enhanced version by her granddaughter Rosalind Webster Perry). Quilt historians Ruth Finley and Florence Peto collected and wrote about quilts, thus saving many bits of women's history and many of their works of art that might otherwise have disappeared.

A woman named Scotio Danner set up a business in the depths of the Great Depression and employed a number of women to travel to large department stores and hold quilting classes, enabling the stores to have a new and expanded group of customers for their "piece goods" departments. Everything, from the new dyes that enabled fabric designers to produce thousands of delightful and colorful cotton prints at a small price to the fact that few women had the money to spend on entertainment outside of the home, made the years of the Great Depression the perfect moment for quilting and for quilt groups as a social outlet.

In 1933, in the very midst of this quilt revival, Sears, Roebuck & Company announced a national quilt contest in conjunction with the Century of Progress Exposition in Chicago. There was a $2000 grand prize and a special $200 bonus prize if that quilt reflected the Century of Progress theme. The pictorial quilts in this category were indeed remarkable but none won the grand prize so the $200 bonus was never given. The total of cash prizes was $7,500, a tremendous incentive at a time when many Americans eked out a living on $1.00 a day! The talent that was unleashed by this contest and the unusual category for pictorial quilts was indeed an inspiration for other women to try their hands at design and to produce quilts not made from the daily newspaper patterns.

As World War II engulfed the minds and time of most Americans in the 1940s, quilting was not as important. In spite of this fact there are many war-inspired and patriotic quilts from that time, most of them original in design. Fabric, however, became scarce and only a few American women had the time to make quilts. After the war most people entered a new world of mass-produced homes, frozen food, and factory-made bed coverings.

It was again a birthday celebration for the country, the Bicentennial in 1976, as well as Jonathan Holstein and Gail van der Hoof's landmark exhibition, *Abstract Design in American Quilts,* at the Whitney Museum of Art in New York in 1971 that brought about another quilt revival with a whole new audience. With improved transportation and communication this new quilt interest began to spread worldwide. Many of the Bicentennial quilts were pictorial and sparked a revival of such quilts that has widened in the ensuing years. Not only has quiltmaking increased in this time but collecting and associated scholarship have risen to heights that would have been hard to imagine in the centuries before 1976, and it seems that the end of this interest is not yet in sight. Though the interest is now worldwide, quilts have developed as a uniquely American art form and through them American life can often be studied.

Today millions of people around the world are making and collecting quilts, and museums create exhibitions around them. They are now known as significant works of art and the prices for museum-quality quilts have soared. Pictorial quilts are often at the top end of the market. The highest known price to date was paid at Sotheby's New York, in October 1991, when a Civil War pictorial quilt brought $240,000 plus a 10% buyer's premium. Though quilts being made today will not sell for such prices for a long time, they are being collected by museums and are being shown in prestigious galleries as works of art. More than anything else they still provide an artistic outlet for many people who find fabric an enjoyable medium.

My interest in collecting nineteenth and twentieth century quilts began in 1977. There are no quilts in my family. It was my interest in art that initially drew me to quilts, first as paintings. My background includes a study of art history and fifteen years as a board member and then chairperson of the Louisville Visual Arts Association, one of the oldest arts organizations in Louisville.

In 1977 my husband and I built a contemporary house. I have always loved contemporary art, especially minimalist art, and I realized I was going to need big art for our big walls. I began bringing home pieces to try out – my husband disliked most of them!

In the fall of 1977 I was invited by two women whom I knew through my children's school to see a col-

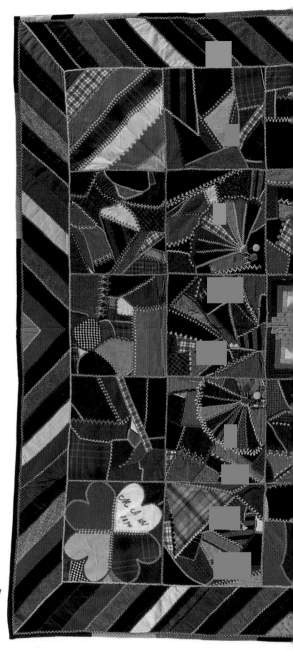

Wool Crazy Sampler, signed and dated MAH 1894, Kentucky. Collection of Shelly Zegart

lection of quilts belonging to a young man from Louisville. He bought Kentucky quilts and sold them in New York and California. It was at this small wine and cheese party that I fell in love with quilts. As Bruce Mann began pulling them out of big black garbage bags, I

at them for the first time, I saw them as paintings.

The Log Cabin quilt that I bought from him that evening still hangs over the fireplace in my living room. I haven't taken it down for many years! I know that conservationists will say that this is not good for it but I have to have this quilt in this spot! It centers me. It reminds me of my introduction to quilts.

When I began The Kentucky Quilt Project in 1981, my growing interest in the history of the women who made quilts and the times in which they lived ignited the focus of my collecting. Today that focus is primarily on pictorial quilts – personal messages spoken by quilters as folk artists. Many of them have accompanying stories and letters which connect me directly to the quilts in my collection and to the women who made them. I would love to have known the maker of every quilt I now own. I would have sought her out for her creative spirit, intelligence, talent, and often, humor.

When I moved to Kentucky in 1968, little did I know that my connections to other women would dramatically expand through quilts. I understand now that my first interest in pictorial quilts was about intimacy. My quilts are story quilts with *real* history and *real* stories. They speak to my heart and the women who made these quilts reach out to me. Most of the pictorial quilts in this book have come from my personal collection. Others are quilts I wish I could own for at least a little while.

I hope that as you read this book and look at these pictorial quilts, you too will become absorbed in their stories, and find personal connections with their makers. Quilter Mary Clare Clark has created twelve wonderful story panels from these old quilt masterpieces. I am sure that her unique interpretations will inspire all quiltmakers to embark on their own personal story quilts.

knew I was hooked. That evening was like magic. I dreamed of quilt images the entire night and had a restless sleep. I did not know anything about them historically or culturally but I loved them! Before that evening I had not even known that they existed, so when I looked

CENTENNIAL ALBUM QUILT

Appliqué and embroidery
78 1/2 x 79 1/4 inches, c. 1876-1880, North Adams, Massachusetts •
Members of the Burdick-Childs family • Shelburne Museum, Vermont

Quilts and quilting and especially the designing of quilts had always been an important part of American home life but in the Centennial Year, 1876, originality blossomed as never before. The citizens of this 100-year-old nation celebrated with such verve and excitement that the images created more than a century ago are still easy to find and recognize in the museums of today. Without such clear proclamations as the words, "Declaration of Independence – Centennial Anniversary – 1776-1876," it would still be possible to understand the patriotic meaning of this quilt.

A unique feature of the 1876 Exhibition was the Women's Pavilion, which the makers have accurately depicted in the second block of the the third row. The Woman's Pavilion was devoted exclusively to exhibits of "woman's labor" with examples of all possible types of needlework and other domestic activities.

This quilt is a fascinating historical document of Victorian domestic life. The makers have painstakingly and with great artistry cut and sewn from a wonderful array of fabric scraps, the art, architecture, and preoccupations of the period.

The makers display a marvellous ability to deal with architectural perspective, and several blocks are dedicated to the exploration of this difficult design element.

Along with learning the finer points of needlework, young Victorian women were taught basic drawing and design skills. The relish in which they tackled this problem is most obviously displayed in the second block of the first row.

They use printed and directional fabrics with great ease: pinstripe shirting provides an ideal wall paper, a rich red paisley is perfect choice for a bedroom carpet, a meandering Greek pattern is a playful solution for a picture frame, and a variety of plaids and checks work well for window panes.

Beyond great artistry and imagination, the contributors epitomize the high standard of needlework skills necessary to execute a quilt of this complexity.

Though many of the designs that appear in the 36 wonderfully busy blocks could have been taken from illustrations in books, magazines, or brochures of the time, there was still much artistic skill required to adapt them so that they fit the exact space and requirements of a quilt. Appliqué designs must have some bold forms and the details must make the picture come to life in simple embroidery stitches. Even finding the appropriate fabrics takes time and a keen artistic eye. Last but not least, a quick sense of humor pulls the story together.

PRETTY POLLY

FOUNDATION AND BACKGROUND

1· Following the *General Directions,* press and fold the foundation square to give you positioning lines.

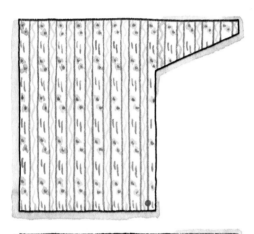

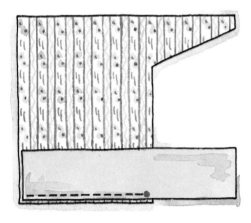

MATERIALS

*Plain fabric for foundation
18 x 18 inches
Striped fabric for floor 18 x 5 inches
Floral stripe for wallpaper 16 x 13 inches
Dark print for door frame 13 x 7 inches
Blue floral for dress 8 x 5 ¹/₂ inches
Brown floral for chair and window frame
10 x 8 inches
Gray print for window and door
13 x 10 inches
Assorted scraps for dog, boy's clothes, and parrot
Eyelet scrap for lady's bonnet and cuffs
Brown bias tape for perch
White bias tape for door jamb
Fusible interfacing
Stranded embroidery floss*

2· From the enlarged pattern, trace and cut out the wall and floor. Mark the seam allowance.

3· With right sides together, sew the wall and floor together up to the marked seam allowance. Press the seam toward the floor piece.

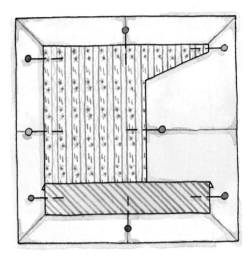

4· Pin the wall and floor unit to the foundation, matching the centers and outside points.

ADDING THE DOOR FRAME

1· From the enlarged pattern, make a template of the door frame. Trace around the template on the shiny side of the fusible interfacing and cut out. Fuse to the wrong side of the door frame fabric and cut out leaving a seam allowance all around.

2· Turn under the seam allowance along the top and left side of the door frame. Cut away the inside of the frame leaving a $1/2$ inch seam allowance.

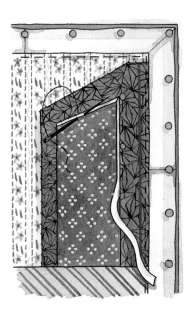

6· Cut a 16 inch piece of $1/2$ inch wide, white bias tape in half lengthwise. Starting at the top left corner, slip the raw edges under the frame. Continue across to the right corner, turning with a neat miter down to the bottom of the frame. Slip the end under the floor piece. This insert will add a three-dimensional perspective to the picture.

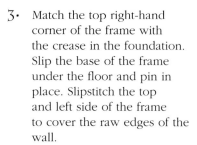

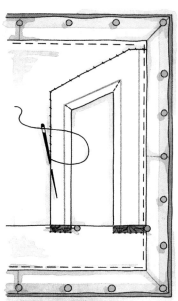

3· Match the top right-hand corner of the frame with the crease in the foundation. Slip the base of the frame under the floor and pin in place. Slipstitch the top and left side of the frame to cover the raw edges of the wall.

4· Baste the right edge of the door frame to the foundation.

5· Snip into the corners of the frame, and turn the inside edges under.

7· Pin the frame and bias through both layers, then slipstitch around the three sides of the frame and along the floor.

PARROT AND PERCH

1· Cut a 16 inch piece of brown bias tape in half lengthwise. Starting from the center top of the arch, pin the curve down the side to the bottom left-hand corner, with the raw edges on the inside of the curve. Leave a section unstitched, and mark with pins to allow the parrot to be slipped under the perch.

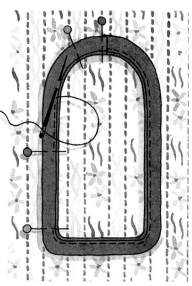

2· Stitch the perch down with small running stitches just off center, toward the raw edge. Overlap the starting point slightly.

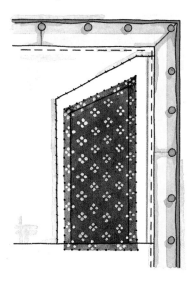

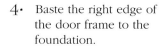

6· Carefully tuck the door inside the frame, making sure all the raw edges are covered by the frame and floor.

3· From the enlarged pattern, prepare a template, cut out, and apply fusible interfacing to the wrong side of the fabric for the parrot and wing. Embroider the parrot's eye before applying interfacing. Cut out both pieces without adding a seam allowance. Pin the wing in position on the parrot.

PICTURE (APPLIQUÉ) SHAPES

4· Slip the parrot/wing unit **under** the left side of the perch, and pin in place. Stitch in place with a small running stitch just off-center. Slipstitch the bias fold over the raw edges of the perch all around the inside.

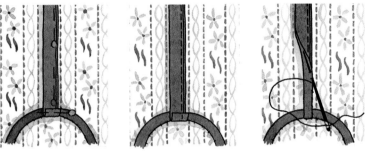

5· Prepare the pole by folding the end of the bias back over itself and covering the join in the arch of the perch. Stitch in the same manner, with a running stitch, just off-center, then, fold over and slipstitch to the background.

6· Pin the parrot's head in place **over** the right side of the perch, and stitch the parrot and wing to the background with a blanket or button-hole stitch.

1· From the enlarged pattern, prepare templates and cut out fusible interfacing for the remaining picture shapes. Trace around the templates placed face up on the right side of the fabrics selected for each design element. Transfer all embroidery details to the fabric shapes.

2· Thread a needle with two dark and one light strand of embroidery floss. Stitch the lady's hair with satin stitch. Use stem stitch for the nose, hand, and sleeves. For the eyes, use satin and couched stitch, and for the mouth, use couched stitch alone. For the facial features, use only two strands of embroidery floss

Embroider the boy's features using the same stitches.

3· Use satin and couched stitch for the dog's eye and nose; stem stitch for the ear and legs.

4· Apply fusible interfacing in the correct position to the wrong side of the dog fabric, the woman's gown, bonnet, window frame, chair, and the boy. Cut out each piece adding a scant $1/4$ inch seam allowance. Press the seam allowances under in preparation for appliqué.

5· Prepare the window frame, cutting away the interior to allow for inserting the "glass panes" using the same reverse appliqué technique as for the door frame. Turn under the four sides and slipstitch to the background.

6· Pin the boy in position on the door. His boots should be placed at the line where the wall and floor meet. Slipstitch the boy to the door.

7· Sew the woman in position on the chair. Use the scrap of eyelet for the bonnet and cuff.

8· Sew the dog to the background.

FINISHING THE PANEL

Refer to the *Stitch Directory* for detailed illustrations of embroidery stitches.

1· Use two strands of embroidery floss to outline each character's face with stem stitch.

2· For the window frame and chair seat, use three strands of floss to stem stitch around the shapes for added surface detail.

3· Use couched stitch for the parrot's feet.

A CURIOSITY BEDSPREAD

Appliquéd and embroidered cotton
74 x 75 inches, 1935, Duck Hill, Mississippi • Made by Mrs. Avery Burton •
Collection of Shelly Zegart

This unfilled summer coverlet was made in the depths of the Great Depression for the Sears, Roebuck & Company "Make-It-Yourself" contest. The entry form and a green merit award ribbon are still attached to the edge. There are also two descriptive lines embroidered along the bottom by the proud designer-maker. One reads, *"Made by Mrs. Avery Burton, Duck Hill, Miss. Age 68 yrs."* Beside it is the following, *"A curiosity bedspread made of Sears, Roebuck & Co. goods in 1935"*, an important notice to the judges, no doubt. In the light of history, two parts of this are interesting: that a woman would not sign her own first name and that Sears, Roebuck & Company no longer carries dress fabric.

The central figures in the bedspread probably represent the farmer and his wife, dressed in their Sunday best. Around them are not only all the farm animals and fowl – horses, cows, chickens, ducks – but trees with vines and berries, and butterflies surrounding the blocks and decorating the border. As in many quilts of the 1930s, embroidery is important to accentuate the figures and finish the edges.

The women of the early twentieth century who made such remarkable pieces of folk art usually did not consider themselves to be artists. They were accustomed to spending their few leisure hours in some useful occupation such as sewing or tending the garden. However, the lure of cash prizes during hard times brought enormous numbers of entrants to quilt competitions.

A CURIOSITY BEDSPREAD,
MADE OF SEARS ROEBUCK & CO.
GOODS IN 1935.

MADE BY MRS. AVERY BURTON,
DUCK HILL MISS.
AGE 68 YRS.

FARMYARD

FOUNDATION

1· Cut a square, 18 x 18 inches for your foundation.

2· To prepare the foundation, press and fold the square to give you positioning lines, then stretch it over a frame as explained in the *General Directions*.

BACKGROUND

1· From the cream fabric cut two squares, each 8 1/2 x 8 1/2 inches.

2· From the brown plaid cut two squares, each 8 1/2 x 8 1/2 inches.

3· Using a 1/4 inch seam allowance, sew the squares together to give you a 4-patch background.

4· Center and baste the 4-patch background to the foundation using the positioning lines previously marked as a guide.

MATERIALS

Plain white or cream fabric for foundation
18 x 18 inches
Cream print fabric 17 x 8 1/2 inches for two
background squares
Brown plaid fabric 17 x 8 1/2 inches for two
background squares
Assorted fabric scraps for animals:
Large cow, 4 x 6 inches
Small cow, 4 x 5 inches
Hens, 6 x 8 inches
Pea hens, two scraps 5 x 5 inches
Pigs, 6 x 7 inches
Chicks, two scraps
Red accents for hen
Fusible interfacing (optional)
Stranded embroidery floss

PICTURE (APPLIQUÉ) SHAPES

NOTE: Decide on the appliqué method best suited to the shapes you will be sewing, as this will affect the way in which you prepare your shapes for cutting. Refer to the *General Directions* to review your options.

1· From the enlarged pattern make templates for all the farm animals.

2· For each shape, place the template face up on the right side of the fabric and accurately trace with a sharp pencil leaving at least 1/2 inch between shapes. Trace around one piglet and one chick

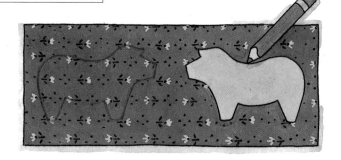

with the template face down on the right side of the fabric, for the mirror image of the shape. The pencil line marks your seam allowance and your sewing line. Transfer all embroidery details to the shapes.

3· Using three strands of embroidery floss, embroider the ears, feathers, and animals' limbs using stem stitch. Use satin stitch for the noses, and French knots to detail the eyes, referring to the *Stitch Directory*.

4· If using interfacing, trace around the template on the shiny side of the interfacing, and cut out each shape to the finished size.

5· Fuse the shape to the wrong side of the fabric in the correct position.

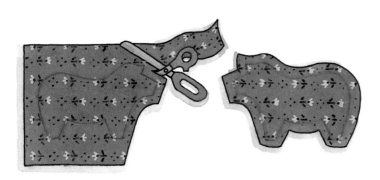

the inside of the legs and the tail or the points of the ears. These tight areas are best done by using the needle-turning method of appliqué, stroking the seam allowance under with a needle, after pinning in position.

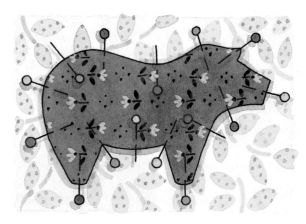

6· Cut out the shapes adding a ¹/₄ inch seam allowance all around.

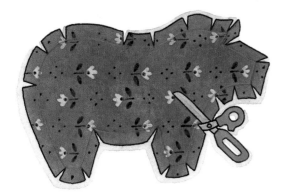

9· When all the animals have been prepared, pin them in position on the background fabric following the detailed directions for pin placement in the *General Directions*.

7· Clip into the seam allowance, especially around curves and into the valleys.

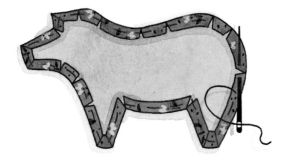

10· The narrow seam allowances that have **not** been basted under require special preparation. For the points of the ears, fold and fingerpress the point down, then fold in the two sides of the triangle.

8· Turn the seam allowance under and baste in place. When starting to baste, put the knot on the right side of the fabric so the basting stitches can be easily removed after the shapes have been sewn. Do not baste the very narrow seam allowance like

11· When pinning the narrow valleys, place the head of the pin into the background at the top of the slit, **not** into the piece being applied. With the pinhead facing the appliqué, and the point of the pin along the slit, the seam allowances are then stroked under with a needle and pinned in place ready to sew.

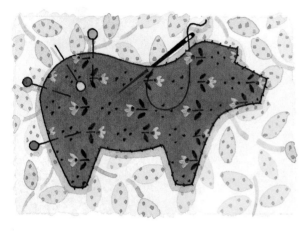

12· Using thread to match the shape being sewn, slipstitch each animal in place.

FINISHING THE PANEL

After the block has been pieced and appliquéd, use three strands of embroidery floss in contrasting colors to the fabric shapes to provide decorative details. For illustrations refer to the *Stitch Directory*.

1· Use feather and herringbone stitches to conceal the seams of the 4-patch background block.

2· Couch down long straight stitches in red thread to detail the hens' feet.

3· Use three strands of embroidery thread to stem stitch the pigs' tails.

Photo: Courtesy of Shelly Zegart

NOAH'S ARK

Pieced and appliquéd wool and flannel
71 x 79 inches, 1900, New York • Quiltmaker unknown •
Inscribed lower right corner: "For Daniel, Love Grandma" • Private collection

The imaginative center panel depicting Noah herding his animals near the Ark was obviously planned to amuse a child and perhaps to teach him his Bible lessons. The dove and the rainbow make it evident that the Ark had landed safely. Such cheerful moral tales were a part of all children's books and room decorations of the time.

The crazy pieced border was a style of patchwork that had its heyday at the turn of the century. It was most often worked in silk and velvet and overlaid with embroidery but in its most utilitarian form, as seen here, it might be of wool and flannel or a variety of cottons such as shirting. It certainly makes a colorful and active frame for the childlike rendition of the well-loved Noah's Ark story.

THEY CAME TWO BY TWO

FOUNDATION

1· Cut a square, 18 x 18 inches for your foundation.

2· Following the directions for foundation preparation in the *General Directions*, press and fold the fabric square to give you positioning lines.

BACKGROUND

1· From the enlarged pattern make templates for the sky, middle ground and lower ground.

2· Trace the shapes onto the right side of the fabric and cut out adding a $1/2$ inch seam allowance all around.

3· Piece the layers together working from the sky downward. With right sides together, match and pin the two outside edges together. Sew the bottom of the sky to the top of the middle ground, easing the pieces as you go along on the $1/2$ inch seam line. Press the two pieces with the seam allowance toward the middle ground.

4· Sew the lower ground to the middle ground following the same steps.

5· Center, then pin the landscape to the foundation using the positioning lines as a guide.

6· Machine stitch the top of the sky to the foundation.

MATERIALS

Plain white or cream fabric for foundation
18 x 18 inches
Beige print fabric for sky 16 x 10 inches
Brown plaid for middle ground
16 x 10 inches
Brown and white pin dot for lower ground
16 x 7 $1/2$ inches
Assorted fabric scraps for animals:
Green print for elephants and deck of ark
Light orange print for hens
Dark orange print for Noah's robe
and upper level of ark
Red print for cats
Green scrap for olive leaves
Yellow print for dove and hens' legs
Tan print for giraffes
Pale brown fabric for Noah's headdress
and hull of ark
Cream scrap for Noah's face and hand
Fabric scraps for elephants' ears and tusks
Two pieces of cord for elephants' tails 3 $1/2$ inches
Black bias tape, $1/2$ inch wide for crook and roof of
ark 12 inches long
Red, orange, yellow, green, blue, and purple
bias tape, $1/2$ inch wide, for rainbow
each 6 inches long
Stranded embroidery floss
Fusible interfacing

PICTURE (APPLIQUÉ) SHAPES

1· Enlarge the patterns provided, and make templates for the ark, giraffes, dove, olive leaves, cats, hens, elephants, Noah, and rainbow.

2· Trace around the templates face up on the right side of the fabric. Transfer all embroidery details to each shape.

3· Use two strands of embroidery floss and the following stitches for Noah's face and hand: satin stitch and couched stitch for

Fold back the middle and lower ground until the top seam can be seen. Pin and stitch the seam allowance to the foundation to make sure the sky is flat. Press. Repeat for the middle to lower ground seam.

7· Pin the bottom edge of the lower ground to the foundation. Machine stitch the sides and bottom of the background to the foundation.

8· Stretch the prepared background in a frame as described in the *General Directions*, ready for the appliqué.

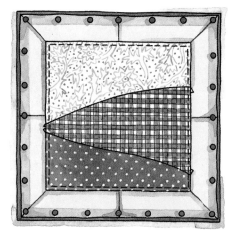

eyelids; stem stitch for his nose and brows; couched stitch for his mouth and long and short stitch for his beard. For the beard, thread your needle with two brown strands and one beige for added texture.

4· Using three strands of embroidery floss, satin stitch the elephants' eyes. Use French knots for the cats' and birds' eyes; stem stitch for the bird's wing, chickens' feathers, and camels' mouths; satin and couched stitch for the camels' eyes and noses; and couched stitch for the elephants' feet.

5· Trace around the templates onto the shiny side of the fusible interfacing and cut out shapes on the pencil line.

6· Place the interfacing shapes in the correct position on the wrong side of the fabrics for each picture item and fuse.

7· Cut out the shapes adding a $1/4$ inch seam allowance all around. To prepare for appliqué, fingerpress the seam allowances under around the edge of the interfacing.

8· Pin the elephants' ears and tusks in place on the prepared shape. Position and pin the giraffes, cats, and hens in place, then slipstitch each animal to the background.

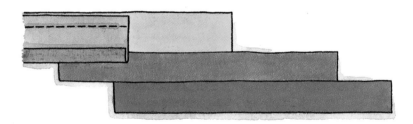

9· To make the rainbow, cut one 6 inch length of bias tape from each of the six colors.

(a) With right sides together, pin the red and orange strips together so that they are offset by 2 inches. Machine stitch along the fold of the bias tape, then press the seam open. Repeat for the other colors, continuing to stagger the strips.

(b) When all the pieces are sewn, pin the ends to an ironing board. Dampen the rainbow with spray and press a gentle arc following the curve of the pattern.

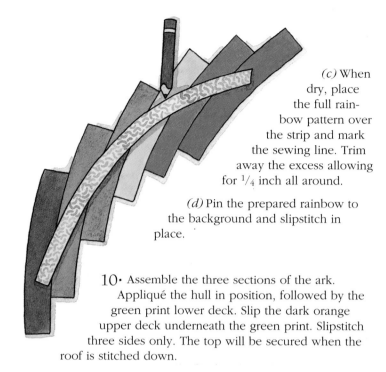

(c) When dry, place the full rainbow pattern over the strip and mark the sewing line. Trim away the excess allowing for $1/4$ inch all around.

(d) Pin the prepared rainbow to the background and slipstitch in place.

10· Assemble the three sections of the ark. Appliqué the hull in position, followed by the green print lower deck. Slip the dark orange upper deck underneath the green print. Slipstitch three sides only. The top will be secured when the roof is stitched down.

11· To make the roof, take a length of bias tape $1/2$ x 4 $1/2$ inches and cut off one of the folded edges.

(a) Press the piece flat and refold it in half. This gives you a piece that is the exact width for the roof.

(b) Pin the tape above the seam allowance on the top of the ark and covering the ends of the rainbow.

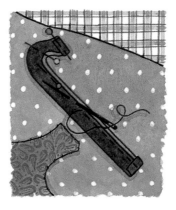

(b) Pin the crook in place along the open edge of the tape, including around the curve of the crook. Fold back the top end and stitch along the length of the tape, slightly off-center toward the raw edges, with a small running stitch, making sure that both the edges of the tape are sewn down.

(c) Turn the lengthwise folded edge over the raw edges, pin to the background, and slipstitch the folded edge.

14· Tuck Noah's hand under the hem of his sleeve and on top of the crook. Slipstitch to the background.

(c) Turn the ends under and stitch along the tape near the raw edges. Turn the tape over and slipstitch the fold over the top edge of the ark.

12· Pin Noah's robe to the background, then slip the face under the neckline of his robe. Finally, pin the headdress in position. Slipstitch all around Noah, leaving the hem of his sleeve open.

13· To make the crook, cut a length of bias tape $1/2$ x $7 1/2$ inches in half lengthwise.

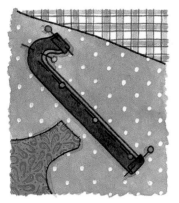

(a) Pin the bottom in place with the lower edge folded back on itself.

FINISHING THE PANEL

Refer to the *Stitch Directory* for detailed illustrations of the following decorative embroidery stitches.

1· For the chickens, use satin stitch for the cockscomb; French knots for eyes; and couched stitch for feet.

2· For the elephants' tails, use cord couched down $1/4$ inch from the frayed ends.

3· Stem stitch the dove's olive branch and stems.

4· For the camels' tails, use couched stitch.

5· Use stem stitch to detail the fingers on Noah's hand.

APPLIQUÉ BEDCOVER

Linen and cotton, appliqué and embroidery
105 x 84 inches, c. 1800, Greenfield Hill, Connecticut •
Made by Sarah Furman Warner • Henry Ford Museum, Greenfield Village

The Warner family of New York produced several outstanding quiltmakers including Sarah Furman Warner and her cousin, Phoebe, and Ann, later in the century. Sarah's Greenfield Village quilt is of cotton, covered with appliquéd and embroidered flowers, birds, people, animals, and houses. The center pictorial block is much like the one on her cousin Phoebe's quilt, now in the collection of the Metropolitan Museum in New York.

The Greenfield quilt has two levels of pictorial images. The larger scene is in the village, with men, women, horses, carriages, and dogs promenading to church. Wonderful abstract trees adorn the scene and birds fly in the sky above the church steeple. Above the village scene is a smaller pastoral scene with a windmill and men, women, and their horses going up the hill toward the pasture filled with sheep and goats.

Both the inner and outer border are lavish with cornucopiae and vases filled with flowers and vines. The use of the applied triangle border, also called "Van Dyke Scallops" or "Dog's Tooth," around the outer edge can be found on other quilts of the period and also on ladies' dresses.

There is barely a spot on the whole surface that is not covered with incredible pictorial appliqué and embroidery. Few families can boast of such exquisite quilts as those made by the Warners.

OUT WALKING

FOUNDATION AND BACKGROUND

1· Following the *General Directions* for foundation preparation, press and fold the 18 inch square to give you positioning lines.

2· Center the background fabric on the foundation and baste around the outside edge.

MAKING THE HOUSE

1· From the gold fabric, cut a rectangle 5 x 8 inches. Cut two strips, ³/₄ x 5 inches for the sides of the house.

2· Mark the position of the windows, doors and stitching lines for the pleats onto the house foundation

MATERIALS

Plain white or cream fabric for foundation 18 x 18 inches

Pale plaid fabric for background 16 x 16 inches

White for house foundation 5 x 5 inches

Gold print for house 5 x 10 inches

Brown print for roof ³/₄ yard russet bias tape, ¹/₂ inch wide for windows, door, chimney

Green print for trees

White scraps for windows/door interior

Brown prints for men's boots and tree trunks

Bright print scraps for breeches, saddle, hats, hair, gloves, and woman's dress

Navy print for horse and men's jackets

Plaid scrap for dog

¹/₄ yard black bias tape ¹/₂ inch wide for cane

Knitting needle, size 2

Fusible interfacing

Stranded embroidery floss

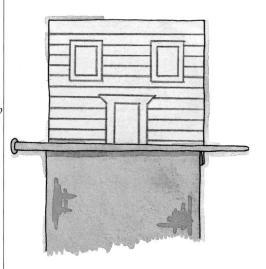

4· Lift the house fabric, insert the knitting needle, and roll the fabric to cover the first stitching line.

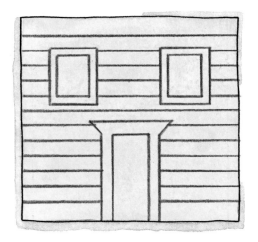

square. This can be done by taking a copy of the enlarged pattern and tracing the lines onto the fabric with a hard pencil.

3· Match the lower and side edges of the support fabric with the house fabric, right sides up, and sew across the first pencil line.

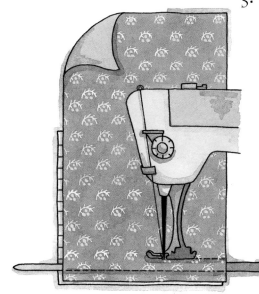

5· Reposition the house fabric on the support fabric and stitch along the second line. Use a zipper foot on your sewing machine to get close to the knitting needle when stitching. Remove the knitting needle and press the pleat toward the lower edge, covering the previous sewing line. Repeat this until all the pleating lines have been sewn.

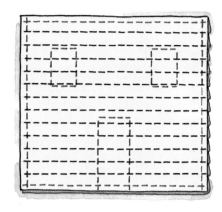

9· For the windows, cut a 7 inch piece of russet bias tape and press in half lengthwise. Fold the end back on itself and pin to the center top of the window opening, with raw edges even.

6· Turn the fabric over to the wrong side and machine staystitch all around the perimeter of the house, door, and windows. Trim the excess fabric away from the sides of the

house close to the stitching. Cut the fabric away from the inside of the windows and door.

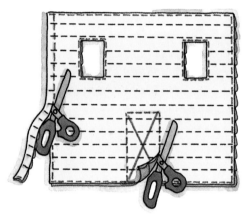

10· Machine stitch around the window with an $1/8$ inch seam allowance. Overlap the fold at the start by at least $1/4$ inch and cut away excess bias tape.

11· Fold the tape over the stitching line, mitering each corner, and turn under the raw edges. Repeat for the other window.

12· Using a 10 inch piece of russet bias tape, prepare the door following the same procedure as for the windows.

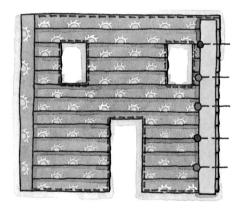

13· Pin the house in position on the pale plaid background. Slip a white square under each window opening and the door. Slipstitch all around the inside of the door and window openings.

7· With right sides together, pin the side strips to the house. Use a $1/8$ inch seam allowance and sew close to the staystitching. Press.

8· Cut out the roof, and apply fusible interfacing. Press seam allowances under along the top and sides of the roof. Sew the roof to the house along the top stitching line. Press.

14· Turn under the top and sides of the chimney and slip it under the roof. Turn under the sides and base of the house and appliqué in place.

PICTURE (APPLIQUÉ) SHAPES

1· Prepare templates for the figures, animals, and trees from the enlarged pattern. Trace around the shapes directly onto the shiny side of the interfacing. Cut out the interfacing shapes and set aside.

2· Trace around the templates on the right side of the fabrics chosen for the picture shapes. Transfer all embroidery details.

3· Use three strands of embroidery floss to embellish the shapes. For the figures' eyes and gloves, use satin stitch. Use stem stitch for the fingers, and couched stitch for the mouth, the trousers, and the top of the cane. Use only one strand of thread to couch stitch the eyelashes. For the beard and hair, use long and short stitch. Use satin stitch for the horse's eye and nose. For the dog's nose, use satin stitch; couched stitch for the eye and mouth; and stem stitch for the ear.

4· Apply the fusible interfacing in the correct position on the wrong side of the fabric. Cut out, adding a scant ¼ inch around each edge of every piece. Press seam allowance under in preparation for appliqué.

5· Pin the saddle and harness in position on the horse, then stitch the horse to the background. Stitch around the saddle and harness last.

6· Appliqué the tree trunks and trees to the background in position around the house. Appliqué the dog and figures, including their hats and boots.

7· Use the technique described for Noah's crook, in *They Came Two by Two*, to prepare and stitch the man's cane.

8· Trace around the dress template on the right side of the fabric and cut around the outside edge. Trace around the three separate dress pieces onto the shiny side of the interfacing and cut them out. Fuse the interfacing to the wrong side of the dress fabric as indicated in the pattern.

9· Clip into the curves and valleys, including the broken line from the shoulder to the point of the triangular piece in the center. Do not clip along the bottom edge. Working on the right side of the dress, gently fold the plain fabric over the fabric stiffened by the interfacing. Pin the fold in place at the top and bottom.

10· Move the top of the piece on the left side over the slit, turning the inside edge down to a point along the hem. Pin down the left side of the dress, turn under the bottom edge, and gently fold the fabric under to create the pleated three-dimensional effect as before.

11· Appliqué the turned-under edges of the prepared dress to the background with a slipstitch.

FINISHING THE PANEL

1· With two strands of embroidery floss, stem stitch around the faces.

2· Use three strands to stem stitch the horse's reins.

BIBLE QUILT

Wool, appliqué with silk and cotton, cut solid velvet, some stamped,
some embroidered with silk in cross, double running, overcast, and satin stitch,
couching, edged in plain weave velvet.
73⅞ x 76⅞ inches, c. 1880, United States • Quiltmaker unknown •
Art Institute of Chicago

The Victorian preoccupation with both biblical stories and embroidery have come together on this decorative quilt. The period from the end of the Civil War until the turn of the century saw great changes in quilts and needlework techniques. Made for decorative rather than for practical use, this quilt is testimony to the increased leisure time for artistic pursuits. Resplendent with elaborate gold embroidery work, it has the charm of crazy quilts of the period. The availability of extravagant fabrics such as silk and velvet made it possible for the average woman to experiment with different materials. Fine threads for embroidery were readily available in local department stores.

The Bible quilt was a popular genre of quilt design amongst Victorian needlewomen. The dominant themes represented here are the familiar tales from the Old Testament: David and Goliath, Daniel and the Lion, and Samson chained to the temple pillars. There are, however, New Testament elements such as Joseph leading Mary on the donkey and the Good Samaritan rescuing a traveler along the road.

The pictures face in four directions, with the Ark drawing focus to the center of the quilt. The border frames the design with a procession of animals carefully inset within each scallop. And, no matter which way the quilt hangs, there is something to look at.

ADAM AND EVE IN THE GARDEN

FOUNDATION AND BACKGROUND

1· Cut a square, 18 x 18 inches for your foundation.

2· Following the directions for foundation preparation in the *General Directions*, press and fold the square to give you positioning lines.

3· Stretch the foundation square across the frame and secure with thumbtacks.

4· Center the background on the foundation, matching the centers and corners with the creases. Pin in place and baste on all four sides.

PICTURE (APPLIQUÉ) SHAPES

Prepare templates for each motif in the panel from the enlarged block pattern.

1· With the templates face down on the wrong side of the fabric, mark the outline of Adam and Eve. Use this tracing for placement of the interfacing. On the right side of the fabric, transfer all details that will be embroidered.

2· Place the fabric in an embroidery hoop. Using three strands of embroidery floss, satin and couch stitch Adam's and Eve's eyes; use couched stitch for the mouths; long and short stitch for the hair and stem stitch and French knots for the hands, arms, legs, and breasts.

3· Use satin stitch for the dog's nose, couched stitch for its eyes and mouth, and stem stitch for the legs and ear.

4· For the bird's eye, use satin stitch. For the wing and beak, use stem stitch.

5· Trace the shapes of Adam and Eve onto the shiny side of the interfacing. Cut out along the pencil line and fuse to the outline previously marked on the wrong side of the fabric.

6· Cut the fabrics out adding a ¼ inch seam allowance.

MATERIALS

*Plain white fabric for foundation
18 x 18 inches
Tan pindot for background fabric
16 x 16 inches
Print fabric for Adam and Eve
7 ½ x 4 inches each
Green prints for trees
Brown plaid for dog
Check fabric for rabbits
Blue print for bird's body
Yellow plaid for bird's tail
Assorted fabric scraps for apples
½ inch bias tape for bird's legs
and head feathers
Fusible interfacing
Stranded embroidery floss
Cotton batting
Knitting needle or crochet hook*

7· Pin shapes in position and slipstitch to the background. Do not sew Eve's left hand down until after the apple has been stitched in place.

8· Trace two fig leaves onto interfacing, cut out, and fuse onto the wrong side of your chosen fabric. Cut out without a seam allowance and blanket stitch into position.

9· Trace the trees, bird, rabbits, and dog onto interfacing and cut out. Fuse onto the wrong side of your fabric and cut out without adding a seam allowance.

10· Position and pin all the above motifs on the background, and blanket stitch with matching embroidery floss.

11· To make the bird's legs and head feathers, use lengths of narrow bias tape, following the directions for Noah's crook in *They Came Two by Two*.

TO MAKE THE APPLES

The apples are made using trapunto, a technique of stuffing the pieces to give a raised effect.

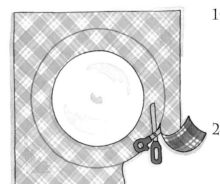

1· Make two sizes of circular templates, for the small and large apples. Cut 13 paper templates with the large circle, and nine paper templates with the small circle.

2· From the assorted red and yellow fabric scraps, trace 13 large apples and nine small apples adding a scant ¼ inch as you cut each circle.

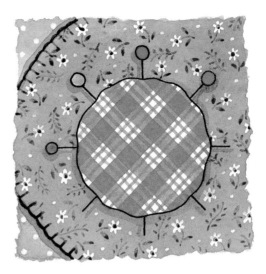

3· Stitch a row of gathering stitches around each circle.

6· Pin the apple shapes to the trees and slipstitch leaving a $^1/_4$ inch opening.

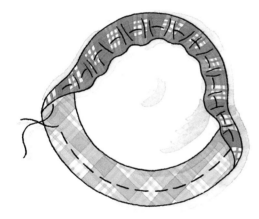

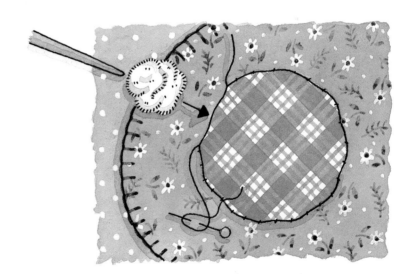

Using a paper circle as a guide, gather the seam allowance around the paper template and tie the thread ends together. Press the folded edge.

4· Take the papers out and pull the gathering threads a little, so that the centers are slightly puffed up. Reserve one of the smaller apples for Eve, but do not stuff it.

5· Slip Eve's apple under her left hand, and appliqué it to the background. Slipstitch her hand to the apple.

7· Secure the sewing thread with a pin and stuff the apples with tiny scraps of cotton batting, using a knitting needle or crochet hook. Do not over-stuff the apples or you will find that the trees and background will become distorted, and cause the fabric to wear.

8· Stitch the opening closed and anchor the stitches securely to the back of the square.

MOTHER-IN-LAW QUILT

Cotton appliqué
83 x 70 inches, c. 1930, Missouri • Made by Lulu Newcomb Bennett •
Collection of Shelly Zegart

Lulu Newcomb Bennett, the maker of this light-hearted quilt was born in 1885 in rural Heralds Prairie Township in White County, Illinois. A local celebrity, she was known as a skillful seamstress as well as a song writer, poet and designer of amusing quilts. A towering house, a patient dog and a feeble-looking mother-in-law making her way up the garden path, capture the humor and imagination for which Lulu Bennett is remembered by those who knew her.

This quilt was made for her daughter-in-law after she heard a joke on the radio that went like this: One man said to another, "I cut off my dog's tail this morning." The other man said, "What did you do that for?" The first man said, "Because I don't want him wagging his tail, showing how happy he is, when my mother-in-law comes to visit." Rarely do we have so much information about what inspires someone to make a quilt, and it is refreshing to know that inspirations can come from such a variety of sources.

Worked in "Municipal" green against a warm gray sky, Lulu's fabric choices are an excellent indicator of popular colors of the period. The simplicity of the appliquéd and embroidered design is enhanced by the cross-hatch quilting in the entire background. The prairie point border, made by carefully folding squares into small triangles and inserting between the layers of the quilt was a fashionable way of finishing quilts in the first half of the twentieth century. A discreet sign at the foot of the path reading, "*The home that tenderly greets the mother-in-law*" adds a playful and personal touch to the quilt.

The home that
tenderly
greets the
mother-in-law

ALONG THE GARDEN PATH

FOUNDATION AND BACKGROUND

1· Cut a square, 18 x 18 inches for your foundation.

2· Following the *General Directions,* press and fold the foundation square to give you positioning lines, then stretch it over a frame.

3· For the background, cut a square 16 x 16 inches. Using the crease-lines on your foundation for positioning, center the background on the foundation and baste in place.

PICTURE (APPLIQUÉ) SHAPES

1· From the enlarged pattern, make templates for the picture shapes.

MATERIALS

*Plain white or cream fabric for foundation
18 x 18 inches
Beige check for background 16 x 16 inches
Gray print for house 6 x 6 inches
Medium brown for house   6 x 6 inches
Brown plaid for house 6 x 6 inches
Blue print lady's dress 4 x 6 ¹/₂ inches
Brown print for garden path
Plaid for dog
Green print for trees
Assorted scraps for flowers, tree trunks, hat,
and basket
Fusible interfacing (optional)
Stranded embroidery floss
Zigzag sewing machine*

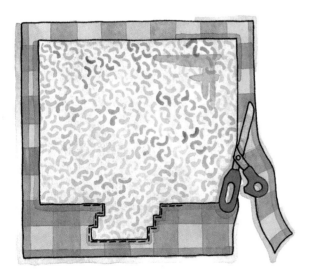

2· Starting with the house, trace the house foundation onto interfacing, cut out, and fuse onto the wrong side of the brown

plaid fabric. Straight stitch around the steps only and cut out the fabric next to the interfacing.

3· From the same fabric, make the chimneys in the same way with a straight stitch on both sides of the pieces.

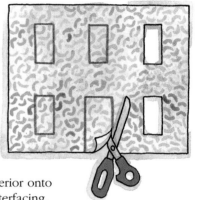

4· Trace the house exterior onto a piece of fusible interfacing. Mark placement lines for the windows and doors. Cut out the shape and the openings for the windows and door by making a small slit in the center and working out to the corners. Trim around the edges, leaving just enough for the frames to overlap. Fuse to the wrong side of the medium brown fabric.

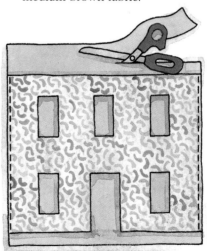

5· Machine stitch down both sides of the house, then cut out adding a ¹/₄ inch seam allowance only to the top and bottom for the roof and steps to overlap. Cut out fabric inside windows and doors leaving ¹/₄ inch allowance to attach the window frames to the building.

6· Trace the window frames, steps, and chimney tops onto the shiny side of the interfacing. Cut out the shapes to include the inside of the door and windows. Fuse onto the wrong side of the gray print fabric. Straight stitch around the outside of all these shapes. Cut the fabric out next to the stitch line and inside the windows and door.

7· Trace the roof onto interfacing, cut out, and apply to the gray print fabric. Cut out the fabric along the interfacing. Pin the roof edge over the top of the house and zigzag along the join.

8· Pin the window and door frames onto the house and zigzag the outside edges around each, including three sides of the door.

9· Slide the brown plaid fabric under the house exterior and pin all the layers onto the background. Baste the layers together so they do not move while sewing.

10· Slip the chimney pieces under the rooftop edge and place the steps and the lower edge of the house on the background. Some of the pieces are quite small so it may be a good idea to baste them first.

11· Zigzag stitch over all the edges of the house, steps, and chimneys, leaving long thread ends to be anchored onto the back.

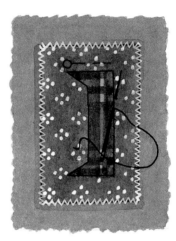

12· To finish the house, turn under the inside of the window frames, pin in place, and slipstitch.

13· Trace the garden path onto the shiny side of the interfacing, cut out, and iron to the brown print fabric. Machine stitch along the edges and cut out the fabric along the stitching line. Pin in place and secure with zigzag stitching along the edges.

14· Trace the dog onto the interfacing and cut out. Trace the shape onto the right side of the plaid fabric. Embroider the nose with satin stitch, the ear and legs with stem stitch, and the eye and mouth with couched stitches. Fuse the interfacing to the wrong side of the fabric and cut out, adding a 1/4 inch seam allowance. Turn under raw edges, pin to the background, and slipstitch in place.

15· Repeat the same process for making the lady, remembering to embroider **all** details before applying the interfacing. Use satin stitch and couched stitches for her eye, couched stitch for her mouth, long and short stitch for her hair, and satin stitch for her glove.

16· Apply interfacing to the wrong side of the lady's hat, turn raw edges under, and appliqué in position.

17· Cut out and appliqué the handbag. Use stem stitch to outline the handle and rim.

18· To make the trees, trace the shapes of the leaves and trunks onto the shiny side of the interfacing, cut out, and fuse onto the wrong side of your fabrics.

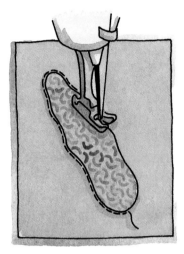
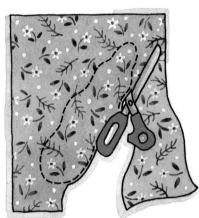

19· Straight stitch around the edges of the trunks and leaves and cut out the shapes near the stitched line.

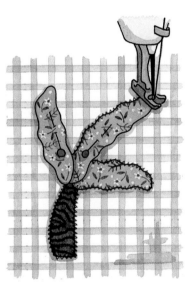

20· Pin the trunks and leaves to the background and zigzag around the outer edges. Take the long thread ends to the back and anchor them so the stitches do not unravel.

21· Prepare the pieces for the small flower patch at the front of the panel with fusible interfacing, and stitch to the background using machine appliqué as for the trees.

22· To make the flowers along the path:

(a) Using templates A, B, and C, cut three circular paper templates. Trace around template A on the red print, B on the pink print, and C on the yellow print. Add a ¼ inch seam allowance around each circle as you cut.

(b) With a running stitch, stitch around the circumference of each circle, leaving long thread ends. Place the paper circles on the wrong side of each circle and pull both ends of the gathering thread, to make circles the same size as the paper templates. Tie the thread ends to secure the shape and press flat. Carefully remove the paper templates.

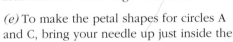

(c) Center the pink circle, B, on the right side of red circle A and center yellow circle, C, on the pink circle. Pin all layers to the background.

(d) To secure the flowers to the background start at the center. Stem stitch or back stitch a small circle inside circle C with 2 strands of embroidery floss. Then stitch a line ¼ inch from the outer edge of circle A.

(e) To make the petal shapes for circles A and C, bring your needle up just inside the stitched circle and go down into the fabric behind the outer edge, dragging the fabric to the inside of the stitching. This will gather the outer edge and create a three-dimensional flower petal. Go over the first stitch at least once more to secure the gather. Repeat this stitch sequence around circles A and C at regular intervals.

SUNDAY SCHOOL PICNIC

Cotton, pieced and appliquéd with embroidery
84 x 82 inches, 1932, Nazareth, Pennsylvania • Made by Mrs. Jennie C. Trein •
Collection of Shelly Zegart

T hirty years after the event, Mrs. Jennie Trein described her award-winning quilt in a letter to the 1964 Dutch Folk Festival: "I can truly say my own designing of the Picnic Quilt is the only one in the whole wide world and therefore very special."

She was inspired to make this enchanting pictorial quilt while on a visit to a friend in the country – "I looked out into the orchard where there was a home-made table from which we ate the world famous cooking of the Pennsylvania Dutch, such as Snitzen Knepp, Rival Soup, home-cured ham and beans ... Then and there my thoughts ran into space. To design and make, (for myself) a Sunday School Picnic Quilt." On a foundation of blue and green fabrics, Jennie Trein has appliquéd and embroidered a joyful and innocent summer event. She has filled her canvas with playful vignettes and charming domestic details. A parade of 40 jaunty Sunbonnet Sues step out around the quilt border following the road sign "To the Picnic." No two girls are dressed alike. Each coat and hat is cut from a different fabric and their accessories are trimmed with extraordinary and loving detail.

The quilt is filled with rural Pennsylvania icons: the church, the graveyard, the log cabin, the well-tended garden, and the beasts of the air and field that furnish the central motif – the table of plenty.

BY THE BOATING LAKE

FOUNDATION

1· Cut a square, 18 x 18 inches for the foundation.

2· Press and fold the foundation square to give you positioning lines as explained in the *General Directions.*

BACKGROUND

1· Using the pattern provided, transfer the embroidery designs for the stars, birds, and windmills onto the sky fabric.

MATERIALS

*Plain white or cream fabric for foundation
18 x 18 inches
Beige print fabric for sky 7 x 16 inches
Ground A - 8 x 6 inches
Ground B - 16 x 11 ¹/₂ inches
Ground C - 16 x 5 inches
Assorted fabric scraps for tree, boys' clothes,
girls' dresses, dog, and bunny
Fusible interfacing
Stranded embroidery floss
Gold metallic sewing thread*

---

directions marked on the pattern. The eyes and beak are embroidered with seed stitch.

For the stars, thread your needle with two strands of yellow embroidery floss and one strand of gold metallic sewing thread.

3· From your enlarged patterns, trace Grounds A, B, and C onto the shiny side of the fusible interfacing.

4· Cut out along the pencil lines and fuse to the wrong side of your chosen fabrics.

5· Cut out the pieces with a ¹/₂ inch seam allowance on all sides.

6· Clip into the hole on Ground B, by making a slit down the center, and clip into the seam allowance.

7· Clip into the top seam allowance of Grounds A, B, and C and press under.

8· Stretch the foundation in a frame and position the sky, matching the center and points of the square with the creases on the foundation and baste in place.

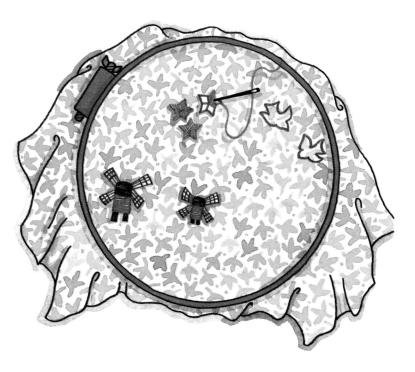

2· Using three strands of embroidery floss, satin stitch the windmills. The sails are made by couching down three lengths of thread. For the birds and stars, use satin stitches sewn in the

9· Position and pin Grounds A, B, and C in place starting with A and working downward.

10· Slipstitch along the turned edges.

11· Baste the outside edges of the background to the foundation.

12· Slip the tree shadow through the slit in Ground B. Pin in place, turn the edges under, and slipstitch in place.

PICTURE (APPLIQUÉ) SHAPES

1· From the enlarged block pattern, make templates for all the picture shapes. Trace around the templates face up on the right side of the chosen fabric. Align the arrows on the tree template with the directional stripes of the fabric before tracing. Transfer all embroidery details to the drawn shapes.

2· Before cutting out, use three strands of embroidery floss to stitch the surface details as follows: use satin stitch for the

figures' hands and shoes and the rabbit's eye and nose; combined satin and couched stitch for the figures' eyes; long and short stitch for the hair, and stem stitch for the hat, dress decoration, dog's mouth, legs, and ear.

3· Trace around the templates of the figures, boats, moon, and animals on the shiny side of the interfacing. Label all the shapes for easy identification. Cut out on the pencil line, and fuse to the wrong side of the fabric. Take special care to fuse the interfacing shapes in the correct position on the wrong side of the embroidered fabrics.

4· Cut out the fabric shapes, adding a ¹/₄ inch seam allowance **only** to the aprons. Do not add ¹/₄ inch seam allowances to the remaining pieces, as they will be appliquéd using blanket/buttonhole stitch.

5· Trace the tree pattern onto the interfacing, cut out on the pencil line, and fuse to the wrong side of the fabric. Cut out the fabric adding a $^1/_4$ inch seam allowance down the center of both pieces. With right sides together, join the tree down the center.

6· Position and pin all the shapes in place with a pin at the top, and bottom and on each side.

7· To secure the shapes to the background, use blanket/button-hole stitch all around the edges with sewing thread in a color of your choice. The decorative stitch on the hem of the gold dress is a closed buttonhole stitch, with white embroidery floss, to create the effect of a lace border. Refer to the *Stitch Directory* for directions.

8· For the patch on the boy's trousers, use satin stitch. Use detached chain or daisy stitch for the apron strings, and stem stitch for the dog's lead.

Embroidery patterns (actual size)

PICTORIAL QUILT

Appliqué and embroidery, felt, wools, and brocades on velvet
94 x 100 inches, c. 1890 • Unknown maker from Mohawk, New York •
Collection of Shelly Zegart

Velvet, felt, brocade, and other decorating fabrics were much used by quilters in the late Victorian period. In this quilt, the appliqué buildings are heavily embroidered, making grill work, stained glass windows, and a Swiss clock stand out with remarkable reality. The bouquets of flowers are built up in layers of wool felt, similar to the technique used in the soldier's quilts of the late nineteenth century. The blocks were made separately and joined, the seams then being covered with a sort of tessellated molding of colored felt.

The strong architectural feeling of the quilt may have come from the fact that the family who made it is said to have gone to Europe to buy furniture and other objects for their grand new home in New York State. Many of the blocks show churches and castles, possibly made from sketches brought back from this trip. There are shields and coats of arms and other distinctive European symbols, along with leopards and lions, possibly taken from paintings. The layered bouquets are pure Victoriana as is the choice of fabrics.

FLORAL FIREWORKS

FOUNDATION AND BACKGROUND

1· Cut a square, 18 x 18 inches for your foundation.

2· Following the directions in the *General Directions* for foundation preparation, press and fold the square to give you positioning lines.

3· Stretch the foundation square across the frame and secure with thumbtacks.

4· Center the blue star background on the foundation, matching the centers and corners with the creases. Pin in place and baste on all four sides.

MATERIALS

Plain white or cream fabric for foundation 18 x 18 inches

Blue Centennial Star fabric for background 16 x 16 inches

White or cream prints for windows, three scraps, each 3 x 5 ½ inches

Brown, rust, and gold prints and gold solid for buildings, each 6 x 6 inches

Assorted pink, yellow, pale blue, navy, and red fabrics, 15 scraps, each 5 x 5 inches

Blue commercial bias tape, ½ inch wide

Blue print scraps for side columns of Building 2

Fusible interfacing

Stranded embroidery floss

Button forms to cover with fabric

special care when handling the sharp points of the towers to fold down the points, and cut away excess fabric before turning under each side.

Building 1

PICTURE (APPLIQUÉ) SHAPES

From the enlarged block pattern, make Templates A, B, C, and G for Building 1, and Templates D, E, F for Building 2. Trace around each template on the shiny side of fusible interfacing and cut out. Mark and cut out each window opening on the **outside** line.

1· Fuse interfacing on the wrong side of your chosen fabric. Cut out adding ¼ inch seam allowances all around pieces B, Br, C, F and G. Add seam allowances to the **sides** only of pieces A and D, and to the **sides** and bottom of piece E. On pieces A, D, and E, cut out the window openings adding ¼ inch around the **inside** of each arch.

2· For Building 1, cut a window insert 3 x 5 ½ inches. For Building 2, cut the bottom window insert 3 x 5 inches, and the top, 2 ½ x 3 ¾ inches. Using these dimensions, cut out three rectangles from fusible interfacing, and fuse to the wrong side of each window insert.

3· Pin the base of Building 1 on the background. Turn under the sides of pieces B, Br, C, and G. Take

Pin in position slipping the bottom edges of B, C, and Br under piece A. Slip the bottom of G under the turned-under edge of dome C.

4· Slip the window insert under the building shape, and baste together ½ inch from the edges and window arches.

Turn under the seam allowances on the inside of the window arches, clipping where necessary to make a smooth curve.

5· For Building 1, cut four bias strips, $^1/_2$ x 8 inches, from the blue print fabric. Fold and press each strip in half, wrong sides together. For Building 2, cut a piece of commercial bias tape 7 inches and another 5 $^1/_2$ inches. Cut each in half lengthwise to make four strips. Use the longer strips for the windows on piece D, and the shorter strips for piece E.

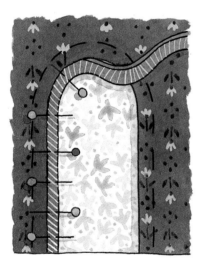

6· Slip the raw edges of the bias strips under the window arches and slipstitch.

7· Cut two strips, $^3/_4$ x 3 inches and two strips, $^3/_4$ x 3 $^1/_2$ inches for the side columns of Building 2. Machine stitch the shorter strips to the sides of piece E, and the longer strips to the sides of piece D. Press. Turn under the raw edges of the columns in preparation for appliqué.

8· Pin the base of Building 2 on the background. Pin piece E in position, slipping the bottom edge under piece D. Turn under the raw edges of the dome, piece F, and center at the top. Slip the base of the dome under the edge of piece E.

9· Slipstitch all turned-under edges of both of the buildings to the background.

BUILDING DECORATIONS

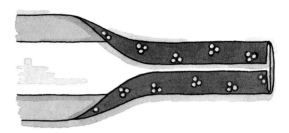

1· To prepare the turrets for Building 2, cut four red print bias strips, 1 x 1 $^3/_4$ inches. Cut another bias strip the same dimensions from the blue print for the center dome. Fold the raw edges into the middle, or use a $^1/_2$ inch strip of cardboard as a pressing template and turn under the ends.

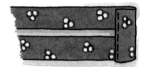

2· Stitch the bias to the top of a blue column. Then gather the tape together $^1/_2$ inch from the bottom, and couch it down to make the first narrow point. Whipstitch twice to hold the gather in place.

3· For the top of the turret, fold the end back on itself, and stitch down. Then gather and couch down another narrow point, whipstitching as before. Slipstitch the turned-under sides and top of the turret to the background.

4· Repeat this technique for each of the remaining four turrets.

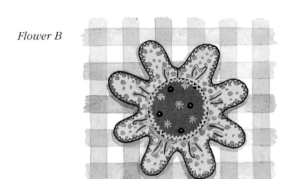

Flower B

Flower C

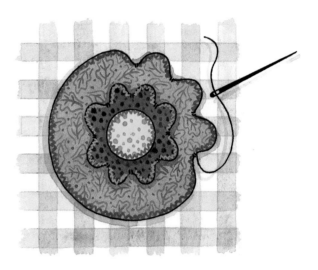

Flower A

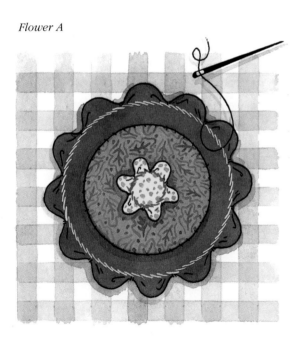

6· Make a small gold print flower to adorn the center tower in Building 1 and a small blue flower to decorate the dome on Building 2.

7· Using the panel as a guide, use three strands of embroidery floss to embroider the base of both buildings with feather stitch. Continue to embroider over the seams in Building 1 with feather stitch. Decorate Building 2 with herringbone stitch. Outline the center turret on Building 2 with stem stitch in bright red thread. Refer to the *Stitch Directory* for detailed illustrations.

8· Following the manufacturer's directions, cover two button forms with gold fabric. Sew the buttons to the tops of the towers in Building 1.

5· Make a colorful assortment of flowers following the instructions for Flowers A, B, and C in *Two Ladies and the Giant Urn*, and stitch to the background.

GRAPE ARBOR QUILT

Appliquéd, embroidered, and pieced cotton
83 x 69 inches, c. 1880, Primrose, Iowa • Thought to have been made by
Marianna Bordecker Hoffmeister • Collection of Shelly Zegart

T he Grape Arbor quilt is an unusual quilt, full of tantalizing details. It is thought to have been made by Marianna Bordecker Hoffmeister who came to America from Westfalen, German in the early nineteenth century.

Pieced in vibrant blues and gold with three-dimensional trapunto work, the quilt in its subject matter and treatment is reminiscent of Middle European folk art. In the main body of the picture, there is little concern for proportion — swans, cows and the grape pickers are all about the same size, while the pensive fisherman, the cascading rose bouquets, the cat tails and grapes are huge in comparison.

The fabrics used to make this quilt are those that were used for clothing and household items in the late nineteenth century — chambray, dark percales and plain white sheeting. The quilt picture has been hand appliquéd and hand quilted, and the irregularities of the shapes suggest that they were most probably cut free-hand. Only the neatly planned and executed lilies on the border have the appearance of having been cut using a pattern. The border has been machine quilted, and the lilies have been sewn over the quilted fabric. Stylistically the border and the central picture are quite different, and indicate that the border may have been added at a later date, or even by another hand.

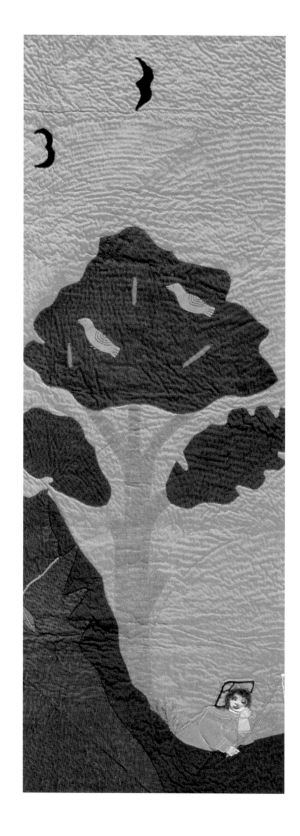

GATHERING IN THE GRAPES

FOUNDATION AND BACKGROUND

1· Cut a square, 18 x 18 inches for your foundation.

2· Following the directions in the *General Directions* for foundation preparation, press and fold the square to give you positioning lines.

3· Stretch the foundation square across the frame and secure it with thumb-tacks.

4· Stitch the water to the ground, slip-stitching around the curve. When this has been done sew the sky to the ground using a $1/2$ inch seam allowance. Press the seam open.

5· Center the sky and ground on the foundation, matching the centers and corners with the creases. Pin in place and baste on all four sides.

PICTURE (APPLIQUÉ) SHAPES

1· Enlarge the pattern and make finished-size templates for the water, leaves, man in sailing boat, animals, urn, and ladies.

2· Trace around the shapes on the shiny side of the fusible inter-facing, and cut out on the pencil line. For one of the ladies, turn the template over and trace, to get the reverse image.

3· Embroider details on all pieces you wish to interface. For the faces, use satin stitch and couched stitch for the eyes; couched stitch for the mouth; stem stitch for the hands and apron strings; long and short stitch for the hair. Use stem stitch for the swan's wing and fish's gill; satin stitch for the eyes. Embroider the veins of the leaves and the detail on the urn with stem stitch.

4· Fuse the interfacing shapes to the wrong side of the fabric cho-sen for each element of the design.

5· Cut out the fish, swan, and leaves using the edge of the inter-facing as a guide. Do not add any seam allowance, as

these pieces will be sewn to the background using blanket or button-hole stitch.

6· Cut out the remaining motifs, remembering to add a scant $1/4$ inch seam allowance around each piece. Fingerpress the seam allowance to the wrong side, to prepare for appliqué.

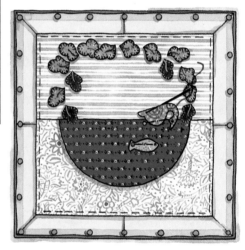

7· Using the quilt as a guide, arrange the grape leaves in an arch, and pin in position. Take care to alternate the fabrics, and allow enough room between the leaves for the bunches of grapes. Blanket stitch the leaves in position.

8· Blanket stitch the fish and swan in place on the water. Use the panel as a guide only. You may wish to alter the arrangement of the fish and swan or even add other elements.

9· Pin the boat at an angle on the water. Slip the man under the top edge of the boat, and baste in position. Slip the man's face under the jacket, and pin the hat in position. Appliqué all around the shapes using a slipstitch. Leave a small gap at the bow of the boat for the mast to be inserted.

10· Baste, and then slipstitch the sail in position around all edges, using the quilt as a guide.

11· To prepare the mast, cut a length of brown bias tape in half lengthwise.

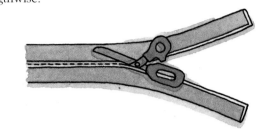

Fold to conceal the raw edges and pin one end to the boat.

12· Prepare a shorter length for the cross piece of the mast. Pin and appliqué in place.

Stitch the mast to the background, overlapping the sail, using the technique used for Noah's crook in *They Came Two by Two*.

13· Pin the aprons in position on the ladies' dresses, then appliqué the ladies to the background on either side of the pond. Leave a small space at the top of each dress, and insert their faces, then finish stitching.

14· Appliqué the urn in position between the women.

GRAPES ON THE VINE

1· From each of two shades of purple commercial bias tape, cut two, 10 inch lengths.

2· From the lilac print fabric, cut two strips, 1 x 10 inches. Fold both raw edges of the strip into the center, with wrong sides facing, and press. Alternatively, fold and press the raw edges of the strips over a $\frac{1}{2}$ inch wide length of cardboard, or use a bias tape maker.

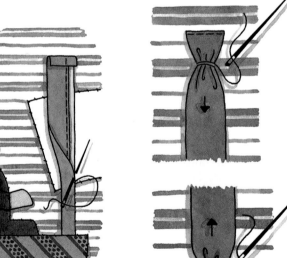

3· Fold the lengths of bias tape in half again, to make a $\frac{1}{4}$ inch wide strip with no raw edges. Start by anchoring the end of one tape to the background, beginning at the lowest point in the bunch of grapes. Move the tape down and couch the tape with several holding stitches to form the bottom of the first grape.

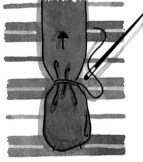

4· Fold the tape back over itself and anchor it at the top with holding stitches.

5· Next, move the tape back down again, and stitch it down along the side of the first grape.

paper, and then pull the gathering threads until the center puffs up.

6· Repeat the sequence, moving the tape up and down, alternating sides, until the bunch of grapes is built up.

2· Place the oval horizontally over the top on the urn. To achieve the three dimensional effect, push the edges in and out to create an uneven, rippled shape. Slipstitch around the irregular outside edge of the grapes. Pin straight down into the fullness of the fabric. Move the ripples around with the pins until the desired effect is reached.

7· To finish off, when the last grape has been stitched down, cut the tape leaving enough excess to turn under the final grape. Stitch the end and then anchor the top fold of the tape with a holding stitch.

3· Start to stitch at the bottom right side of the shape. Couch the fabric down around the pins, using very small holding stitches. Take care not to catch the thread on the pins. If this becomes unavoidable, use a piece of paper to cover the pinheads.

8· If you want a variegated bunch of grapes, use different colors of bias tape, following the same directions. Start at the bottom with one color and introduce the second shade about halfway up the bunch.

4· When the grape has been sewn down, use beads to embellish the shapes and conceal the holding stitches.

GRAPES IN THE URN

1· Using the template, trace an oval from the dark purple fabric. Cut out adding a scant $1/4$ inch seam allowance. Sew a row of running stitches, within the seam allowance, all the way around. Gather the oval over the template. Press, remove the

FINISHING THE PANEL

1· Use detached chain stitch for the apron bows. Outline the hands with stem stitch.

2· Stitch the sailing ropes and the grapevine stems with stem stitch.

3· Embroider the small birds using satin stitch. Use beads for the eyes and in clusters on the background to resemble grapes.

ALBUM QUILT

Appliquéd, embroidered, and pieced cotton
85 x 100 inches, dated August 1854, New York or New Jersey •
Made by Sarah Ann Wilson • Collection of Shelly Zegart

This strikingly handsome album quilt was signed and dated, "Sarah Ann Wilson, August 1854," and consists of thirty elegant blocks of simple floral and figurative motifs, separated with narrow bands of turkey red sashing. The quilt is finished with an unusual border of double scallops with embroidery and eyelets.

All the figures which occupy the middle row of blocks are depicted in black fabric, and gives some credence to the theory that Sarah Ann Wilson was an Afro-American. Another quilt illustrated in Volume 1 of the *American Index of Design*, purportedly by the same maker includes similar figures and suggests that they were probably members of Sarah Ann's family.

Many of the motifs featured, such as the oak leaf, the wreath, bouquets and flower-filled urns are conventional album motifs but Sarah Ann brings to her quilt a simplicity and modernity that sets her work apart from the mainstream of the 1850s. Her stylized and flat shapes are reminiscent of the paper cut-outs made by artists of the twentieth century.

Working with a limited range and palette of fabrics, Sarah Ann has created a very sophisticated quilt, and in the tradition of most album quilts it was probably made for a special occasion.

VASE BOUQUET

FOUNDATION AND BACKGROUND

1· Cut a square, 18 x 18 inches for the foundation.

2· Following the *General Directions*, press and fold the foundation square to give you positioning lines.

3· Stretch the foundation square across the frame and secure with thumbtacks.

4· Center the striped background on the foundation, matching the centers and corners with the creases. Pin in place and baste on all four sides.

PICTURE (APPLIQUÉ) SHAPES

1· Enlarge the design, and prepare a template for the vase and birds. Trace around the templates on the shiny side of the fusible interfacing. Cut out the interfacing shapes.

2· Trace around the bird template on the right side of your chosen fabric. Reverse the template for the bird to face the opposite direction. Transfer the embroidery details, then embroider using satin stitch for the birds' eyes, and stem stitch for the wing detail.

3· Fuse the interfacing to the wrong side of the vase fabric, and in the correct position on the embroidered bird fabric. Cut out the vase remembering to add a scant $^1/_4$ inch all around. Fingerpress the seam allowance under in preparation for appliqué. Cut out the birds without adding any seam allowance.

4· Center the vase in position on the background. Baste, then slip-stitch the vase in place, leaving the top unsewn until after the flowers and stems have been slipped under the edge.

5· Set the birds aside until the floral bouquet has been sewn.

FLOWERS AND LEAVES

NOTE: For this panel, which uses the Broderie Perse technique, (see *General Directions*), you need a good selection of floral print fabrics with large and realistic multicolored shapes. These fabrics can usually be found in drapery or interior design stores, rather than in dress or craft/fabric stores. Select tightly woven, flat-weave cotton. The heavier satin weave is too heavy to turn under and the fine ends poke out when turning, so it is a good idea to avoid this fabric altogether. Cotton fabrics with a shiny chintz finish are appropriate, but some may be a little stiff to sew through.

Use the panel as a guide only. Your picture will be governed by the flower shapes you choose.

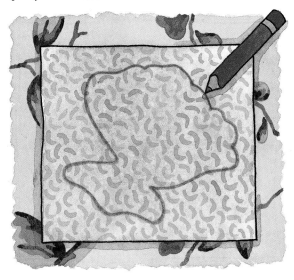

1· When you have chosen the flowers and leaves, place the fusible interfacing directly **on top** of the shape, with the shiny side up. Trace around the flower or leaf shapes, though it is not essential to trace exactly.

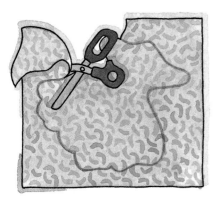

3· Clip into the edges, especially the curves and valleys.

2· Cut out the interfacing on the pencil line, fuse it to the wrong side of the fabric, and then cut out adding $1/4$ inch seam allowance.

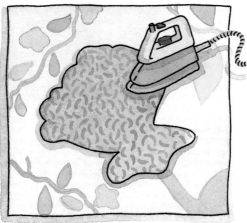

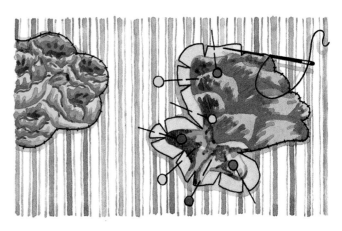

4· Pin the flowers and leaves in place, with at least two or three holding pins, and then use the side of the needle to turn the edges under. Pin the seam allowance under and pin to the background at right angles to the turned-under edge.

STEMS

1· To prepare the flower stems, cut several bias strips from two shades of green fabric, each 1 x 8 inches. Cut a strip of cardboard, $1/4$ x 8 inches to use as a folding template.

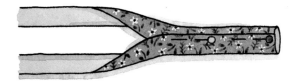

2· Pin the end of the bias strip onto an ironing board with the wrong side up, put the cardboard in the center of the strip and fold both sides over the cardboard.

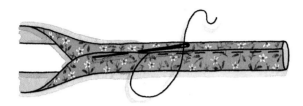

The raw edges will overlap, and you can press the folds in place or baste the edges with a long holding stitch through the overlap only.

3· Slip the cardboard out, and prepare the remaining stems. Store the strips flat so they do not crease by rolling them over a small tube, such as the tube inside of a roll of kitchen towels.

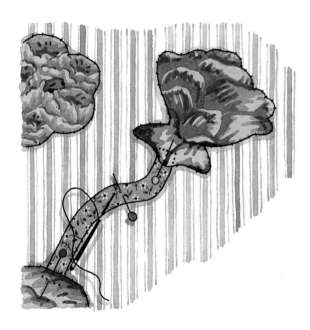

4· Slip the ends of the stems under the flowers and the vase. Pin the curves in place and slipstitch both the edges. Some leaves will be slipped under the edge of the strip and others can be placed over the strip. This will give the stems and leaves a more realistic look.

BIRDS

1· Following the same directions as for the flowers and leaves, prepare the birds for appliqué.

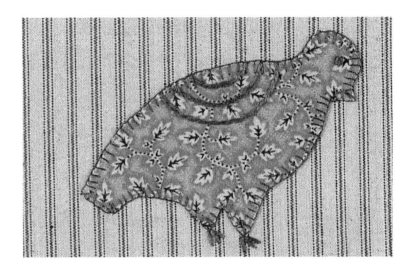

2· Use blanket or buttonhole stitch to sew the prepared birds in position on the background fabric. If you can find fabric with printed birds or butterflies, use the Broderie Perse method as for the flowers.

THE PHOEBE COOK QUILT

Appliqué, piecing, embroidery, and quilting on cotton and silk
75 x 94 inches, 1872, Morrow County, Ohio •
Made by Phoebe Cook • Ohio Historical Society

In 1872 Phoebe Cooper Cook, then in her 68th year, proudly recorded the life around her, block by block and in a long parade around the border of her quilt. She carefully stitched in the date, but even without that useful last touch, the stylish clothes and fine fabrics would make the time period obvious. One especially interesting style is the "Dolly Varden" dresses, named for a character in the then-popular *Barnaby Rudge* by Charles Dickens.

Sandy Fox, in *Wrapped in Glory*, says that Phoebe Cook "had an excellent understanding of the principles of dressmaking." That is not surprising as most women, even those who were not professional seamstresses, made some or all of their own clothes and those for their families. There is a great sense of style in all the clothing and accessories of both men and women as they walk, ride, or drive their carriages around the quilt. Many women at that time read *Godey's Lady's Book* for the fashionable female, and many other publications on fashion.

It has been conjectured that the sashing represents the new railroad that ran through the town of Edison where Mrs. Cook lived on its route from Cleveland to Cincinnati. In its entirety, this quilt provides a lively and energetic depiction of small-town life in America over a hundred years ago.

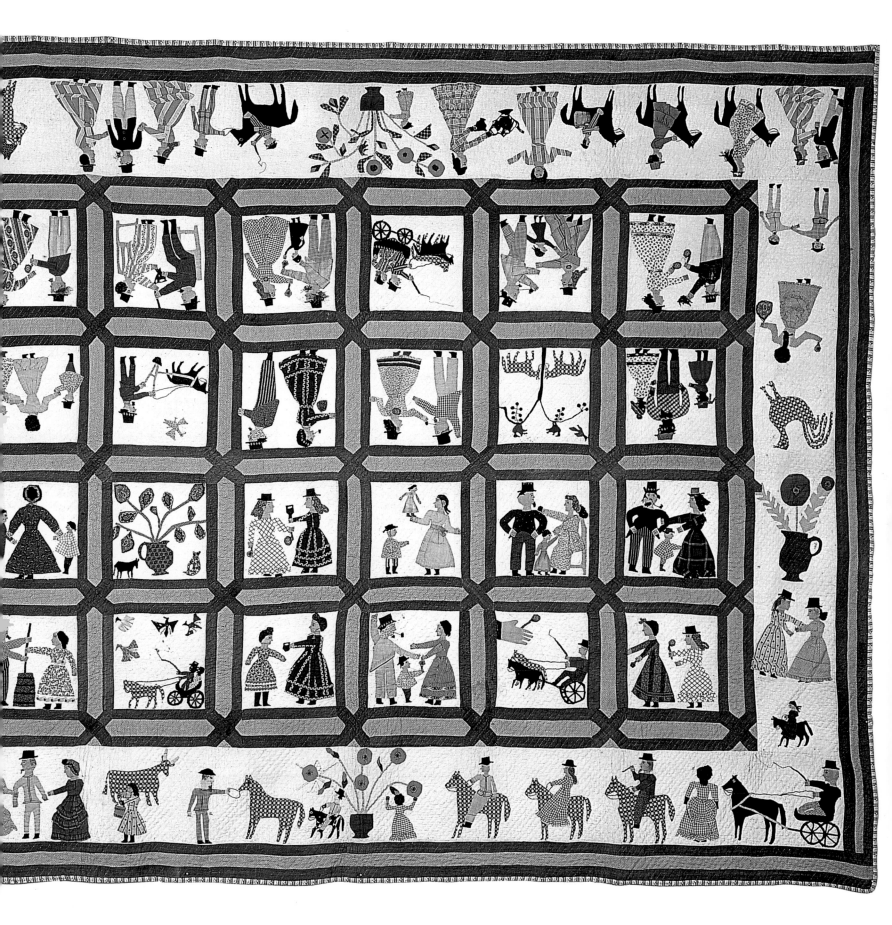

TWO LADIES
AND THE GIANT URN

FOUNDATION AND BACKGROUND

1· Cut a square, 18 x 18 inches for your foundation.

2· Following the directions in the *General Directions* for foundation preparation, press and fold the square to give you positioning lines.

3· Cut a background square, 16 x 16 inches. Using the crease-lines on your foundation for positioning, center the background on the foundation and mount in a frame. Baste around the edges.

PICTURE (APPLIQUÉ) SHAPES

1· Prepare templates for the urn and the ladies from the enlarged pattern. Trace the shapes onto the shiny side of the fusible interfacing and cut out. Remember to place the template face down on the fabric and interfacing for **one** of the ladies to get the mirror image. Apply interfacing to the urn and ladies' dress fabric and cut out, adding a ¹/₄ inch seam allowance. Press the seam allowance under ready for appliqué.

2· Position, pin, and slipstitch the urn in place.

3· Trace around the face template on the right side of the fabric. Transfer the facial details and embroider the eyes using satin and couched stitch, the mouth with couched stitch, the hair with French knots, and the chin outline with stem stitch. Following the pencil tracing, cut out the embroidered faces, adding a ¹/₄ inch seam allowance.

4· Using the same template, trace the faces onto a scrap of fusible interfacing and cut out. Position onto the wrong side of the embroidered face fabric and fuse in place.

5· Position and pin the ladies on either side of the urn. Slip the hands and feet of each figure under the sleeves and hem of the dress. Tuck the heads under the necks of the dresses. Pin the hats on top of the heads.

6· Slipstitch the figures in place.

Plain cream or white fabric for foundation 18 x 18 inches
Beige check for background 16 x 16 inches
Tan print for urn 9 x 9 inches
Red print and green print for dresses/hats 6 x 5 ¹/₂ inches each
Assorted scraps for faces and hands, flowers, and leaves
Fusible interfacing (optional)

TO MAKE THE FLOWERS

(Type A, B, and C)

Flower A

1· Using templates A, B, and C, cut three circular paper templates. Trace around template A on the red print, B on the pink print, and C on the yellow print. Add a ¹/₄ inch seam allowance around each circle as you cut.

2· With a running stitch, stitch around the circumference of each circle, leaving long thread ends. Place the paper circles on the wrong side of each circle and pull both ends of the gathering thread, to make circles the same size as the paper templates. Tie the thread ends to secure the shape and press flat. Carefully remove the paper templates.

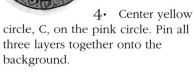

3· Center the pink circle, B, on the right side of red circle A.

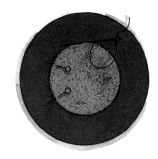

4· Center yellow circle, C, on the pink circle. Pin all three layers together onto the background.

5· To secure the flower to the background, start with the center. Stem stitch or back stitch a small circle inside circle C with 2 strands of embroidery floss. Slipstitch circle B in place, then stitch a line $1/4$ inch from the outer edge of circle A.

Turn the fabric over and zigzag stitch over the straight stitch on the right side.

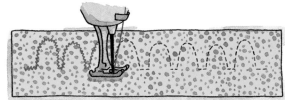

6· To make the petal shapes for circles A and C, bring your needle up just inside the stitched circle and go down into the fabric behind the outer edge, dragging the fabric to the inside of the stitching. This will gather the outer edge and create a three-dimensional flower petal. Go over the first stitch at least once more to secure the gather. Repeat this stitch sequence around circles A and C at regular intervals.

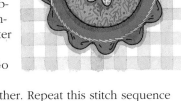

3· Cut out the fabric close to the stitching along the curved edges. When cutting out the bottom edge, add $1/4$ inch to allow for gathering or pleating.

Flower B
These flowers are machine-edged and appliquéd to the background with a zigzag machine stitch.

1· From the template provided, trace the petal unit onto fusible interfacing. Cut out the interfacing along the pencil lines and fuse to the wrong side of the fabric.

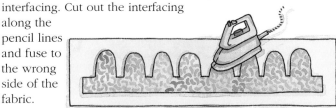

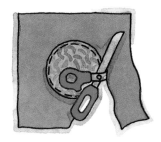

4· Using template C, trace the flower center on the fusible interfacing and apply to wrong side of your chosen fabric. Straight stitch all around the circle, then cut out close to the stitching.

2· Machine straight stitch, on the wrong side of the fabric, along the edge of the interfacing, but not along the bottom edge.

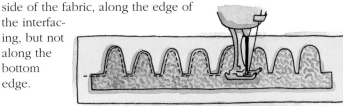

5· Gather or pleat the petals and pin at the center, overlapping the start and finish.

6· Baste, then straight stitch the flower center to the petals.

7· Pin the flower to the background and zigzag around the center. Leave long thread ends to pull through to the wrong side to anchor the stitching.

Flower C

This flower is made with three circles of fabric, each edged with a zigzag stitch.

1· Cut out three different-sized circles from fusible interfacing. Fuse onto the wrong side of your fabrics. Straight stitch all around the outside of each circle. Cut out the smallest circle close to the stitching.

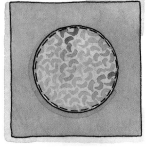

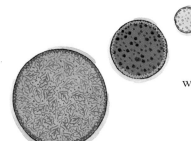

2· Zigzag along the stitching line of the two larger circles. Carefully cut out the circles close to the stitching with sharp embroidery scissors.

3· Layer all the circles together. Place them on the background fabric and baste in place. Zigzag stitch around the inner circle through all the layers, leaving long threads at the beginning and end, to anchor the stitching on the back.

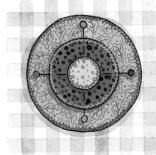

4· To make the petals, bring your needle up under the middle circle catching the zigzag edge of the fabric. Use the needle to pick up a small stitch and pull the thread toward the center to create a gather. Fasten with a small stitch. Repeat at regular intervals all around the middle circle to give you the petal shapes.

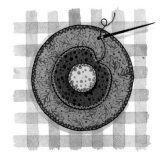

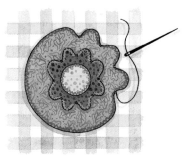

5· Repeat this process for the outer circle, anchoring the flower to the background.

Leaves

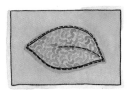

1· Trace the leaf shapes onto fusible interfacing, cut out, and iron to the wrong side of the fabrics.

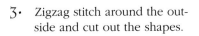

2· Straight stitch the outer edges and down the center stems.

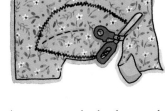

3· Zigzag stitch around the outside and cut out the shapes.

4· Baste to the background. Zigzag stitch down the center stems and extend these stitches onto the background. This technique is also used for the trees and leaves in the panel, *Along the Garden Path*.

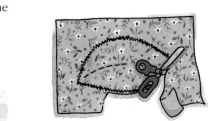

SETTLING OF THE WEST

Cotton pieced, appliquéd, and embroidered
103 x 83 inches • Started March 1930 and completed September 1932 •
Made by Mildred Jacob Chappell • Collection of Shelly Zegart

This prize-winning quilt is an exuberant celebration of America's pioneering spirit. The inscription embroidered in the lower left-hand corner of the quilt reads:

TO THE PIONEER
"VIRILE TO RISK AND FIND, KINDLY
WITHAL AND A READY TO HELP, FACING THE
BRUNT OF FATE: INDOMITABLE, – UNAFRAID."
DONNER LAKE, CALIFORNIA

Mildred Chappell, the maker, has achieved a masterly and simple composition of a slow procession of covered wagons moving westward across the open plains. Small groupings of buffalo, bears, and brave pioneers on horseback and on foot, with bounding dogs at their heels, give a charming innocence to what would have been an experience of considerable hardship. The scenes around the border depict the legendary figure of Geronimo, the explorers Lewis and Clark on their journey to find the Pacific Ocean, the Pony Express, and other great tales of frontier life.

Inscribed on the back of the quilt is "I Mildred Jacob Chappell, made this quilt as a labor of love, Love for the 'Old West' as I have known it in history and books. Love of the 'New West' as I have known it in travel. Love of the Indian before the white man invaded his kingdom. This quilt, which I have called 'The Settling of

OF THE INDIANS
SETTLERS OF THE WEST
BEFORE THE WHITE MAN

FUR STOCKADE ON THE COLUMBIA RIVER

THE LEWIS AND CLARK PARTY

the West,' was made between March 1931 and September 1932. My only regret is that I could not have lived one hundred years earlier to experience those stirring times, instead of only having made this quilt to commemorate them."

A note written by Mrs. Elizabeth McCullah of Yuma, Colorado, May 12, 1934 attached to the quilt confirms its popularity. It reads – "Slabsides, the [Colorado] mountain cabin of Mr. and Mrs. H.V. McCullah was the scene of a very interesting gathering on the afternoon of July 31, 1933, when Mrs. Mildred Chappell assisted by the daughter of the house, Miss. Eunice McCullah, served tea to the guests who came to marvel at the unique design of the quilt and the very skillful workmanship of the maker. During the afternoon about seventy-five people came to call and visit."

WAGON TRAIN

FOUNDATION AND BACKGROUND

1· Cut a square, 18 x 18 inches for the foundation.

2· Press and fold the foundation square to give you positioning lines, then stretch over a frame as explained in the *General Directions*.

3· Center the background fabric on the foundation, then pin and baste around all four sides.

PICTURE (APPLIQUÉ) SHAPES

1· From the enlarged pattern, make a template for each pictorial element.

2· Trace all the shapes onto the shiny side of the fusible interfacing and cut out. When tracing the wheels, the window, and the front opening of the wagon, mark the interfacing with an "X" to identify the areas to be cut out.

3· Transfer the embroidery details to the animals and people. Embroider using two strands of embroidery floss for the noses, eyebrows, and eyelids. Use satin stitch for the eyes, couched stitch for the lids, and stem stitch for the nose. To outline the shirt sleeves and animals' limbs, use stem stitch.

4· Fuse the interfacing shapes in the correct position onto the wrong side of both the plain and embroidered fabrics.

5· Cut out each shape adding a $^1/_4$ inch seam allowance.

6· Clip into the allowance up to the interfacing, especially on curves and in valleys on all shapes.

MATERIALS

Plain white or cream fabric for foundation
18 x 18 inches
Cream print for background 16 x 16 inches
Blue print for sky 10 x 3 $^1/_2$ inches
Brown print for wagon base and one buffalo
8 x 5 inches
Brown plaid for wagon cover and dog
Blue print for second buffalo
Scraps for other appliqué pieces
Bias tape, $^1/_2$ inch wide for horns and yoke
Ribbon for barrels
Fusible interfacing
Stranded embroidery floss

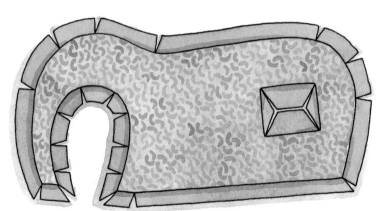

7· To make the windows in the wagon cover and the spokes in the wheels, cut away the center of the space to $^1/_4$ inch from the interfacing. Then cut out to the corners, leaving a triangular shape to be turned under.

If the triangles are very large the points on the seam allowances can be trimmed away.

8· Baste the top and side of the sky to the background then slip-stitch to secure.

TO FINISH THE PANEL

After appliquéing all the shapes, use two strands of embroidery floss in a matching color to stem stitch the animals' tongue and beards. Use couched stitch for the tails and stem stitch for the hands.

9· Pin then slipstitch the two buffalo in place.

10· Before positioning the wagon and cattle on the background, pin the pieces together in the order in which they overlap. Start with the lowest piece and work up from the background, matching the interfacing edges.

11· Pin the wagon unit in position and slipstitch in place.

12· Use bias tape to make the horns and the yoke.

GENERAL DIRECTIONS

In designing each of the twelve picture panels I have considered one main needlework technique. An understanding of each technique will help you in making your own story quilt. For instance, in *Adam and Eve in the Garden,* I discuss how to use trapunto to create three-dimensional apples; in *Out Walking* you will have fun learning how to make a clapboard house with pleated fabric, and in *Pretty Polly* you will have to think about using directional fabric to create perspective.

My design interpretations are just stepping stones along the path to making your own picture quilts. You may choose to add other elements to change the panels, or even adapt motifs from the enlarged details of the old quilt masterpieces that are featured in the book.

On the final page of this chapter there are instructions for finishing one block and for joining up all twelve. Whether you choose to make just one panel, several, or all twelve, I am certain that you will be captivated by the challenge of creating stories in cloth.

GETTING STARTED

In addition to basic sewing equipment, you will need an embroidery frame or a pair of canvas stretchers, thumbtacks, template plastic, medium weight fusible interfacing, and an embroidery hoop. Fabric requirements are listed for each element in the block. If an exact amount of fabric is not specified, then the shape is so small it can be cut from a scrap 5 inches square. Take special care when choosing fabric for appliqué to select closely woven 100% cotton. High quality cotton will stand up to high iron temperatures, holds a crisp edge, and does not ravel easily. The foundation fabric, on which the background of each block is mounted, can be unbleached muslin of lesser quality. For *Vase Bouquet*, which features Broderie Perse, use floral or figurative glazed cotton chintz, even if it is upholstery fabric. For *Pretty Polly*, use directional fabric that is suggestive of wallpaper for the interior of the room and for the floor; cut a linear fabric that is evocative of wood, at an angle for a three-dimensional effect.

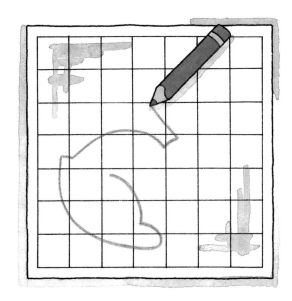

ENLARGING YOUR DESIGN

The block patterns reproduced in the book have been reduced to 9 inches. There are two methods you can use to enlarge the design.

The first is to use a photocopy machine to increase the pattern by 167%. To reduce the possibility of distortion, be sure that the page from the book lies completely flat on the glass plate.

Alternatively, draw a 1 inch grid within a 15 inch square on a large sheet of paper.

Working with the block pattern and blank grid side by side, transfer the design onto the corresponding larger grid, square by square. For curved lines, use a flexible ruler in order to go from point to point on the grid.

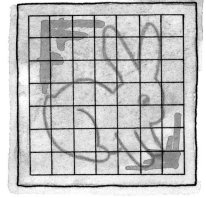

MAKING TEMPLATES

Once you have enlarged the block design, accurately trace each element directly onto transparent template plastic and cut out. If you prefer, use tracing paper to copy the pattern and glue it to heavy cardboard, before cutting out on the pencil line. The pattern you have made is the finished size of the shape and does not include any seam allowance. Transfer all markings, including embroidery designs, to the template, and label with the name of the block design.

Prepare quilting templates following the same guidelines, but remember to cut out interior areas of the design with a sharp craft knife.

MARKING, TRANSFERRING EMBROIDERY DESIGNS, AND CUTTING

As a rule, cut out the largest pieces of your design first. To mark the fabric, use a well-sharpened pencil, dressmaker's carbon paper, or water-soluble marking pencil. Trace around the template, placed right side up on the right side of the fabric, keeping your marking tool against the edge of the template. Leave at least $1/2$ inch between shapes for seam allowances.. For some of the block designs, you will need to reverse the template, placing it face down on the right side of the fabric. This will give you the mirror image of the shape. You will need to use this technique for the piglets in *Farmyard*, *Two Ladies and the Giant Urn*, *Gathering in the Grapes*, and the trees in *Out Walking*.

When using fusible interfacing, trace around each template on the shiny side of the interfacing material, and cut out on the pencil line. To conserve material, place the shapes one against the other without any space in between.

Using dressmaker's carbon, or water-soluble pen, transfer all embroidery details and contour lines to the fabric after tracing the outlines. Embroider all details before cutting out fabric or applying interfacing. Cutting after embroidery helps eliminate the frayed edges that result from handling while hand-stitching.

Transferring embroidery patterns using dressmaker's carbon placed between fabric and tracing paper.

For all appliqué techniques with turned-under edges, add a scant $1/4$ inch seam allowance around each shape as you cut. If you intend to machine appliqué or use buttonhole stitch to secure the shape to the background, then cut out exactly on the pencil line without adding a seam allowance.

PREPARING FOUNDATION AND BACKGROUND FABRICS

The foundation fabric helps to keep the seams and appliqué motifs flat, while supporting the background fabric. Although the finished dimensions of the block are 15 inches square, we will be working on a foundation square of 18 x 18 inches to allow for "shrinkage" that occurs when appliquéing. In addition, because the block will be handled frequently and mounted in a frame, it is liable to ravel. After the appliqué work is complete, the foundation will be remeasured and trimmed down to 16 x 16 inches to include $1/2$ inch seam allowances for sewing the blocks together.

Prepare the plain cotton foundation fabric by folding it in half and pressing to make fold lines. Press in half again, then press the corners back to make diagonal creases from the center to the outside points. The creases are used as positioning lines for the background. Because in appliqué you stitch the pieces in place by working from

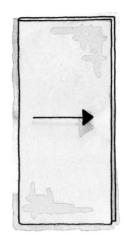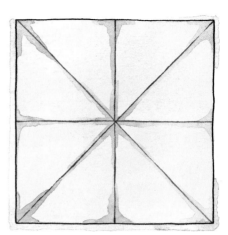

the background to the front, it is essential to create an attractive "landscape" on which to build the appliqué design.

To place your picture shapes on the background exactly as indicated in the pattern, trace placement lines on the background using the enlarged block design. Alternatively, prepare your shapes for appliqué and place them freely on the background according to your preference.

APPLIQUÉ TECHNIQUES

Several appliqué methods have been used to make the fabric pictures in this book. For **hand-appliqué**, use a strand of thread to match the shape being sewn, and slipstitch (or blind hemstitch) the shape to the background. To slipstitch, bring the needle up through the folded edge of the appliqué shape, picking up one or two threads of fabric.

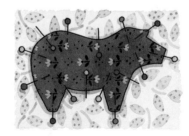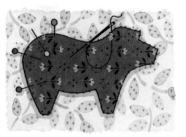

Then take it down through the background just above the spot where it came up. For the next stitch, bring the needle up through the edge of the appliqué shape a scant $1/8$ inch farther on. Taking one stitch at a time, pull each stitch so that the appliqué shape is firmly anchored but not so tight as to cause puckers. Regardless of your chosen appliqué method, do not be afraid to use lots of pins to position your shapes, and keep the seam allowance pinned under. Experiment with pin placement, but generally you will have most success pinning at right angles to the edge of the appliqué shape.

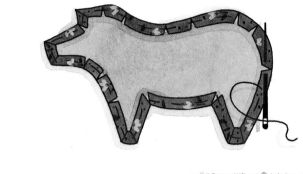

For **traditional appliqué,** clip into the seam allowances as required, fingerpress the seam

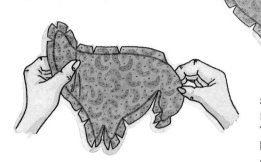

allowance under, pin in place, and slipstitch. This technique works best for large, smooth shapes.

To **needle-turn,** arrange the cut-out shapes on the background fabric. Anchor each shape by basting $1/4$ inch from the edges. This will allow you to turn under a scant seam allowance without having to remove any basting stitches. Working from right to left, turn under the $1/8$ inch seam allowance on the pencil line with the tip

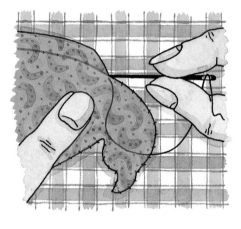

stitch the inside, or concave curves first, before sewing the outside.

To **prepare circles or ovals,** trace around the required template and cut out the shape, adding a scant $1/4$ inch seam allowance. Run a single row of gathering stitches around the fabric shape about $1/8$ inch from the edge. Leave excess thread to gather around the template and tie off. Distribute the gathers evenly around the shape. The paper template helps define the circle and the gathered seam allowance slightly pads the shape.

of your needle. Reverse the sewing direction if you are left-handed. Turn under and fingerpress about $3/8 – 1/2$ inch at a time. Use your needle to "nudge" the seam allowance under when turning a concave curve. For convex curves, turn under the allowance a stitch or two at a time, pressing with both thumbs while giving the edge a slight stretch. This should be enough to curve the seam without having to clip it.

To **pre-baste,** turn under the $1/4$ inch seam allowance on the pencil line and baste. Do not turn under any edges that will be covered by other pieces of appliqué. On tight curves, acute angles or valleys, trim down the seam allowance slightly, making it possible to turn under without clipping, especially on curves where the fabric is cut on a bias. Clip into the seam allowance when necessary and always stop short of the pencil line. When appliquéing curved stems,

For added stability, apply lightweight fusible interfacing, cut the same size as the template, to the wrong side of the circle before gathering. This method is used in *Adam and Eve in the Garden, Gathering in the Grapes, Floral Fireworks, Along the Garden Path,* and *Two Ladies and the Giant Urn.*

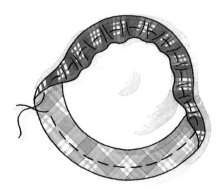

To **prepare sharp points**, trim away some of the excess fabric before turning down the point. Then turn under the sides on the pencil line, one after the other.

side up on the shiny side of the interfacing, and cut out on the pencil line. Fuse the interfacing in the correct position to the wrong side of the fabric. For machine appliqué and hand appliqué using blanket/buttonhole stitch, cut out the fabric along the edge of the interfacing. For hand appliqué with turned-under edges, cut out adding a scant ¹/₄ inch seam allowance all around each shape.

Another way to prepare shapes for appliqué is to **machine staystitch** before cutting out, just outside the pencil line. This stabilizes the edges of the fabric and helps to turn under the raw edges. Cut out the shape adding a scant seam allowance, then clip into the valleys and curved edges up to the staystitched line. Pin the seam allowances under and slipstitch the shape in place.

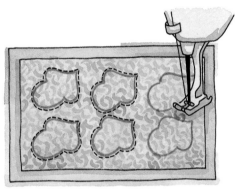

To **machine appliqué**, cut out fabric shapes without seam allowances after applying interfacing and machine staystitching. Using an open zigzag or machine-basting stitch, sew around the shape very close to the raw edge to anchor it to the background. Adjust

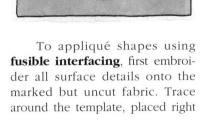

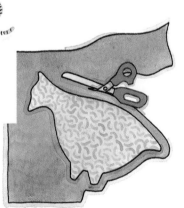

To appliqué shapes using **fusible interfacing**, first embroider all surface details onto the marked but uncut fabric. Trace around the template, placed right

your sewing machine to make a satin stitch, which is a very close zigzag stitch. You will need to practice on a piece of scrap fabric the same weight as the finished item to establish the correct stitch tension so that no bobbin thread shows on the top. Ideally, the bulk of the stitch should cover the appliqué shape to finish the raw edges. At the

Trapunto

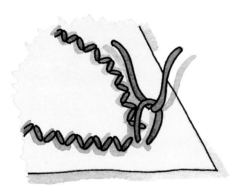

beginning and end of your sewing, leave long thread ends, pull them to the back, and tie them off. *Along the Garden Path* explores many of the possibilities of machine appliqué.

Reverse appliqué is a special technique which involves layering fabric, then cutting away the top layer to reveal the fabric underneath. It is used on the windows and door frames of *Pretty Polly*, for the arches on the buildings in *Floral Fireworks*, and for the tree shadow in *By the Boating Lake*. When cutting away the top layer of fabric, take care not to cut through to the bottom fabric by accident.

Broderie Perse, used for the flowers in *Vase Bouquet*, is an appliqué technique which involves taking printed fabric motifs from glazed chintz, cutting them out, and rearranging them on a plain background to make a new design.

Several different methods have been used in order to give a three-dimensional quality to the blocks. In *Adam and Eve in the Garden*, **trapunto** is used on the apples for added texture. This involves preparing a circle for appliqué as previously described, but gathering up the threads slightly tighter to make the shape puffy. Slipstitch the circle to the background, but leave a small gap in the side through which stuffing can be inserted. Finally, stitch the opening shut.

To give the appearance and depth of a clapboard house, fabric is pleated onto a foundation. For the gentle folds of the lady's dress,

which add texture and movement to the block design, fusible interfacing is applied ingeniously to certain areas of the fabric shape. Details for these techniques accompany the block *Out Walking*.

The flowers which are a prominent feature in *Floral Fireworks*, *Two Ladies and the Giant Urn*, and *Along the Garden Path* combine many different hand and machine techniques to achieve added depth and texture. Study the photographs of these blocks carefully to help you understand the way in which the flowers are created.

Many of the blocks use **bias tape** in unusual ways to create depth and perspective. It is used for the boat's mast, then ruched and couched down to make bunches of grapes, in *Gathering in the Grapes*; for Noah's crook and the rainbow in *They Came Two by Two*; and for the cane in *Out Walking*. Bias tape is inserted between the layers of the reverse appliqué to add a three-dimensional effect to the door frame in *Pretty Polly* and the window arches of *Floral Fireworks*, in addition to being used for the parrot's perch. For the turrets in *Floral Fireworks*, bias tape is gathered, couched, and stitched down to give a clever surface treatment.

EMBELLISHMENTS, EMBROIDERY, AND SURFACE STITCHING

After the appliqué shapes are stitched to the background, decorative elements are used to enhance and embellish the blocks. Beads are used in the ruched folds of the grapes in the urn and seed pearls are used for the birds' eyes in *Gathering in the Grapes*. Eyelet lace trims the lady's sleeve in *Out Walking*, while covered buttons add decorative detail to the towers in *Floral Fireworks*, offering an alternative to an ordinary appliquéd circle.

While most of the embroidery is stitched before the shapes have been interfaced, cut out, and appliquéd, many of the blocks use embroidered stitches as surface decoration. For example, in *Farmyard*

and *Floral Fireworks*, herringbone and feather stitching are used to conceal seamlines, while most blocks use stem stitch to outline shapes. In *They Came Two by Two*, embroidery is used for the hens' feet, the animals' tails, and the olive branch. Refer to the *Stitch Directory* for detailed illustrations of suggested embroidery stitches.

FINISHING

Once you have completed your block or blocks, the raw edges must be finished. You can mount the individual appliquéd block on heavy cardboard, folding and basting the edges to the back, and then frame it. Alternatively, separate multiple blocks by sashing strips and posts, add batting and backing, and quilt. To join all twelve blocks and make up the quilt as shown in the frontispiece, follow the step-by-step directions. The finished dimensions will be 72 x 55 inches.

MATERIALS

12 appliquéd blocks, each 18 x 18 inches
Dark mini-check fabric for sashing 1 yard
Light check for corner posts ¹/₄ yard
Batting 58 x 74 inches
Backing/binding 3 ¹/₂ yards
Quilting thread

1· From the mini-check fabric cut 31 strips, 3 x 16 inches for the sashing.
2· For the corner posts, cut 20 squares, 3 x 3 inches
3· Trim the appliquéd blocks down to 16 inches squares. Arrange them in a grid three across and four down.
4· Keeping the blocks in order, pin and sew three blocks and four vertical sashing strips together, alternating the blocks and the sashing. When sewing blocks and sashing together, use a ¹/₂ inch seam allowance for extra reinforcement.
5· Repeat to make four rows of three blocks each. Press all seam allowances toward the sashing strips.
6· Pin, then sew horizontal rows of four posts alternating with three sashing strips. Repeat to make a total of five rows. Press the seam allowances toward the posts on each row.

7· Sew rows of posts and sashing to the rows of blocks and sashing, taking care to match points by locking opposing seam allowances.
8· Press the completed quilt top carefully. Trim away any loose threads which may show through to the front of the quilt.
9· Tape down the corners of the quilt to a firm surface, and trace the quilting pattern to the sashing and posts. Mark the appliquéd blocks with a design of your choice. Outline quilting of picture images may be sufficient to add just that little bit of texture and depth to each block.
10· Cut the backing fabric in half to make two equal lengths. To avoid having a center seam joining the backing, cut one piece in half, lengthwise. With selvages even, sew the split lengths to either side of the backing using a ¹/₂ inch seam. Trim away selvages, then press the seams to one side.
11· Tape down the backing, right side down, to a flat surface. Center the batting and quilt top on the backing, smoothing out the wrinkles to the edges.
12· Baste the layers together in a horizontal and vertical grid, down the centers of the sashing, and through the centers of each block.
13· Quilt according to your marked design.
14· Trim the batting to leave a 1 ¹/₄ inch excess beyond the raw edge of the quilt top on all four sides.
15· Trim the backing to leave a 1 ³/₄ inch excess beyond the batting on all four sides.
16· To use the self-binding method to finish the raw edges of the quilt, bring the backing to the front of the quilt, enclosing the batting. Turn under ¹/₄ inch and slipstitch the fold to the quilt along the seam allowance, finishing each corner with a neat miter.
17· Quilt along the inside edge of the binding through all the quilt layers to finish.
18· Remove all basting stitches.

STITCH DIRECTORY

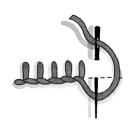

Blanket/Buttonhole Stitch

Double Feather Stitch

Long and Short Stitch

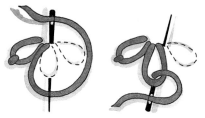

Chain Stitch

Feather Stitch

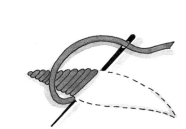

Running Stitch (Quilting Stitch)

Closed Buttonhole Stitch

Fly Stitch

Satin Stitch

Couched Stitch

French Knot

Stitching Hen's Foot using couched stitch

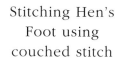

Herringbone Stitch

Stem Stitch

PROJECT: PRETTY POLLY

Each Square = 1 inch

PROJECT: FARMYARD

Each Square = 1 inch

PROJECT: THEY CAME TWO BY TWO

Each Square = 1 inch

PROJECT: OUT WALKING
Pleating patterns for house and dress, see page 127

Each Square = 1 inch

PROJECT: ADAM AND EVE IN THE GARDEN

Each Square = 1 inch

PROJECT: ALONG THE GARDEN PATH
House foundation pattern, see page 127

Each Square = 1 inch

PROJECT: BY THE BOATING LAKE

Each Square = 1 inch

PROJECT: FLORAL FIREWORKS
For various flower patterns, refer to page 125

Each Square = 1 inch

PROJECT: GATHERING IN THE GRAPES
For grapes in the urn, see pattern on pages 125 and 127

Each Square = 1 inch

PROJECT: VASE BOUQUET

Each Square = 1 inch

Flower C

Flower A

Flower B

PROJECT: TWO LADIES AND THE GIANT URN
For flower patterns, see page 127

Each Square = 1 inch

Flower B (center)

Flower B

PROJECT: WAGON TRAIN

Each Square = 1 inch

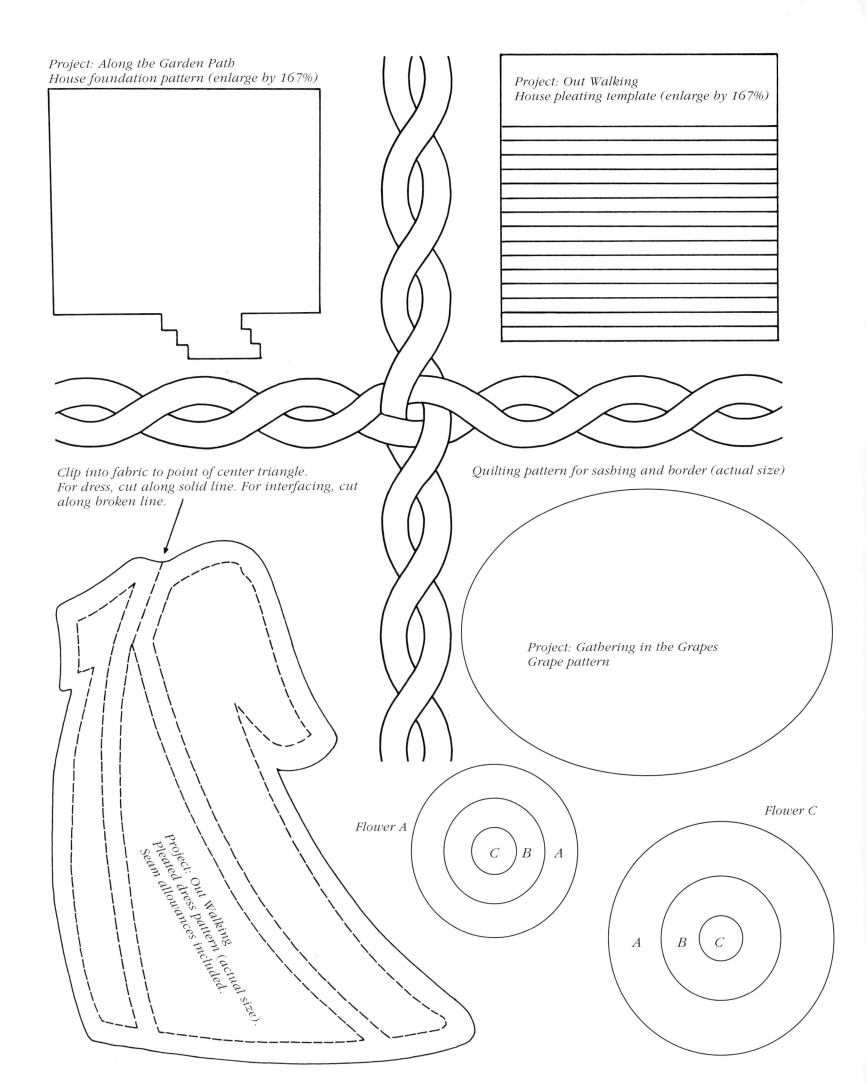

Project: Along the Garden Path
House foundation pattern (enlarge by 167%)

Project: Out Walking
House pleating template (enlarge by 167%)

Clip into fabric to point of center triangle.
For dress, cut along solid line. For interfacing, cut
along broken line.

Quilting pattern for sashing and border (actual size)

Project: Gathering in the Grapes
Grape pattern

Project: Out Walking
Pleated dress pattern (actual size).
Seam allowances included.

Flower A

C B A

Flower C

A B C

INDEX